Healing Through Spirituality

Go on a Healing Spiritual Journey and Reprogram Your Mind to Live a Happier, More Fulfilling Life | The Keys to Successfully Manifesting the Life You Want

Travis Hemingway

© **Copyright 2022 Travis Hemingway - All rights reserved.**

The content contained within this book may not be reproduced, duplicated or transmitted without direct written permission from the author or the publisher.

Under no circumstances will any blame or legal responsibility be held against the publisher, or author, for any damages, reparation, or monetary loss due to the information contained within this book, either directly or indirectly.

Legal Notice:

This book is copyright protected. It is only for personal use. You cannot amend, distribute, sell, use, quote or paraphrase any part, or the content within this book, without the consent of the author or publisher.

Disclaimer Notice:

Please note the information contained within this document is for educational and entertainment purposes only. All effort has been executed to present accurate, up to date, reliable, complete information. No warranties of any kind are declared or implied. Readers acknowledge that the author is not engaged in the rendering of legal, financial, medical or professional advice. The content within this book has been derived from various sources. Please consult a licensed professional before attempting any techniques outlined in this book.

By reading this document, the reader agrees that under no circumstances is the author responsible for any losses, direct or indirect, that are incurred as a result of the use of the information contained within this document, including, but not limited to, errors, omissions, or inaccuracies.

Table of Contents

Introduction 1
   Understanding Spirituality 3
      Defining Religion and Spirituality 4
   My Welcome Message to One and All.................................... 6
Chapter 1 Defining Your Spirituality... 8
   Types of Spirituality.. 9
      Spirituality Models 10
   Believe in Your Faith... 12
      Spiritual Practices.. 14
      The Spiritual Journey Continues 15
Chapter 2 It's All About Your Hidden Inner Treasure Trove......... 16
   Exploring Your Inner Jungle.. 17
      Understanding the Value of Your Treasure Trove.............. 18
   Connecting Your Mind to Your Inner Treasure 21
      Breaking the Molds of Negativity 22
Chapter 3 Altering the Way You Think 25
   Opening the Doors to Your Mind Palace 26
      It's All in the Planning: Altering the Way You Think 28
      Redecorating Your Mind Palace... 30
      Furnishing Your Mind Palace 32
Chapter 4 Don't Be Afraid to Reach for Your Dreams 34
   Becoming Part of the Dream Team—Again 35

Setting Your Dream Goals 36

  The Dream Menu of Success 38

  The Highway to Manifesting Your Dreams 40

Chapter 5 All Things are Possible—The Power of Manifesting Your Dreams and Desires 42

  It's About What You Can Do for the Universe 43

    Clarity Through Contrast: Getting the Results You Desire 45

    Setting Clear Guidelines Based on Your Dreams 46

  Use Your Universe to Reach for the Stars 49

Chapter 6 Giving Your Desire a Voice 50

  The Voice of Reason: Manifesting Awareness and Attention for Your Desires 51

    Give Your Desires the Attention It Deserves 53

    Using the Law of Vibration to Fuel Your Desires 54

  Lean Into Your Desires 56

Chapter 7 No Place for Self-Doubt—Working Towards an Obstacle-Free Spiritual Oasis 58

  Using the Best Friend Code to Manifest the Abolishment of Self-Doubt 59

    Resetting the Self-Doubt to Self-Respect 60

    Reconnecting With Yourself 61

    Removing the Obstacles in Your Way 63

  You be You, and Leave Everyone to Be Whoever They Are 65

Chapter 8 Side-Stepping Your Negative Thoughts 68

  The Implications of Being Encased in Negativity 69

    The Side Effects of Negative Thinking 70

The Importance of Positive Thinking 72
Adopting a Positive Mindset to Assist Negative Thinking 74
Breaking the Negative Thinking Molds 74
The Journey to Reclaim Your Misplaced Focus 76
Chapter 9 Reclaiming the Focus That Was Lost Along the Way 78
Giving Your Focus a Little More Attention 79
Focusing on Keeping Your Focus Where it Is Most Important 80
Manifesting the Shift in Your Focus 81
Chapter 10 Understanding the Essentials of Intention 84
New Rules According to Intention Manifestation 85
Sorting Your Dreams and Desires from Your Intentions 86
The New Faces of Manifesting Intentions 87
Chapter 11 Energy Is the Power which Fuels the Universe that Feeds Your Spiritual Oasis 91
The Power of Energy: Different Types of Energy 92
Mental Energy 93
Soul and Spirit Energy 94
Using the Power of Energy to Find Your Purpose 94
Your Energy Levels 95
Random Acts of Kindness 95
Identifying Your Purpose in Life 96
Identifying Your Purpose in Life: Gut Intuition 97
Conclusion 99
Utilizing the Universal Outpouring of Energy to Create the Life You Deserve 100

Are You Living Your Best Life?... 100

The Stepping Stones to Your Pedestal...................................... 101

Introducing the Gifts From the Comfort of Your Best Life Pedestal 103

All Roads End at the Bubbling Brook 105

References.. 106

Words From the Author

Hey, it's Travis. Thank you so much for giving me a chance to make an impact in your life. I feel its my *mission* to help guide anyone and everyone who is looking for an answer. I find it important that I share what I've learned on my journey thus far. Hopefully, by doing so, you all won't have to feel as lost as I once did. That's all for now and I hope I'm able to help.

As a thanks for your support, I have a **FREE** gift for you. Just scan the code below.

Introduction

Spirituality is recognizing and celebrating that we are all inextricably connected to each other by a power greater than all of us and that our connection to that power and to one another is grounded in love and compassion. Practicing spirituality brings a sense of perspective, meaning and purpose to our lives. –
Brené Brown

- Are you struggling to find a happy medium in your life?

- Are you struggling to let go of things you can't control?

- Are you struggling to let go of the fear that is preventing you from realizing your true purpose in life?

- Are you ready to find that peaceful place in your mind that will allow you to be the architect of your mind, body, and soul?

It doesn't matter whether you've answered yes or no to the questions above because you are right where you need to be. I am not going to shove, cram, or attempt to change or alter anything about you. I would love to promise you that I will leave you as I found you, but that may just make a liar out of me. Don't start up those panic pedals just yet—my statement doesn't mean that I am going to alter anything about you. What I am implying is that you may read something that resonates with how you are feeling in the moment, and incorporate it into your life as we embark on our journey together.

I know what it is like to distrust people. I have been there, and I believe that it is safe to say that we have all been in that little life raft. It is not a very nice place to be, because the distrust affects us in ways that no one can explain. We experience many different types of emotions that we may not understand, and that is normal. We will go through periods where we are flooded with thoughts that are all over the place. Others will just ride the way out to where it will take them. Not everyone has the same experiences. Guess what? It's okay to be different, and unique. I love the idea of being different and unique because I am one of a kind. It took hard work and a lot of convincing for me to implement and embrace the changes that I developed through my journey. You don't have to trust me. You don't have to believe in my motives.

You will know when the tides have changed because it will be at that moment when you will experience a warmth spread through your mind, body, and soul—your *wow* moment. It will come when you least expect it. It may come while you're reading this book, when you're out in the middle of the ocean, or pulling weeds in your garden. Everyone will have a different experience. Embrace your wow moment when it finds you. Don't be despondent if you don't experience your wow moment on command. You can't force yourself to experience your wow moment. Life doesn't work like that. You need to continue living your life, and doing good and I can guarantee that your wow moment will find you. A watched pot never boils. I love this proverb because it's something my mother and grandmother used to say. Your impatience may slow down the time it takes for your wow moment to reach you because you are so busy looking for it, that you are not enjoying the one life you have.

This journey doesn't require airfare, special clothing, or worrying about calories. This is a very special journey that has one very big requirement, and that is for you to have an open mind. I would like you to be open to everything you may encounter on this journey. I would like you to remember that you are not going to be forced to do anything or believe in anything you don't want to. This is a spiritual journey of the mind, body, and soul.

Understanding Spirituality

I have previously mentioned that I am not here to shove or cram anything down your throat. That includes the very delicate topic of religion. I am not here to force you to convert to Christianity, Buddhism, Islamism, paganism, or any other type of religious belief. I am not here to convert you to adopt something you are not comfortable with. Spirituality and religion are very similar, and I do believe that many people get them mixed up. I want to show you that anyone can be part of the spiritual community. Spirituality isn't defined by who or what you believe in, nor is it dependent on your age, gender, or ethnicity. I came across an article penned by Steve Scott for the *Happier Human* online publication.

My research led in many different directions. I found it interesting that people often lumped spirituality and religion together, which is understandable because they are similar. I realized, as I read Scott's article, that society generally shoves you in one direction. I have found that community members are very vocal when it comes to religion. Most of the older generation that I have met are not shy to express their feelings and views about religion. In their eyes, there is no room to wiggle or negotiate between religion and spirituality, and they will not listen to the possibility that the two are very different. I was raised to respect my elders, so I won't be getting into arguments, but I strongly believe that finding yourself on the spiritual plane is important to your long-term health and well-being. Do you need permission to have a different opinion? Do you want someone to tell you that you are on the right path? No, you don't need to justify yourself to anyone but yourself. That is why I am writing this book—I want you to be who you are meant to be, with or without religion, spirituality, and anything else in between.

Defining Religion and Spirituality

Please tag along as I show you the differences between religion and spirituality (with the help of Scott). This little tour is meant to help you understand my intentions. I don't want naysayers whispering in your ear and forcing you to choose sides. This is a decision that rests squarely on your shoulders. No one has the authority to force you into a corner to make a choice. The only choice that is applicable in this scenario is chosen by you because this is your life. Do you want to know what is better than having the freedom of choice? You are not bound to any contracts, you don't pay any sign-up fees, and you are allowed to change your mind a million times until you find what you are looking for. Your perfect fit is just around the corner.

Religion

What is religion, and what does it entail? I'm so happy that you've asked, and I would like to share Scott's findings with you. Religion is an institution made up of practices and beliefs as determined by the various religious denominations. It is based on a system that teaches individuals about the word of God and the writings of prophets in the Bible. Religion is run as an organization or multi-billion-dollar company with a CEO, a board of directors, and employees to ensure everyone is doing what they are meant to be doing. Religious individuals are categorized under the umbrella term known as Christians. These individuals are mostly born into their religion where they are schooled in worshiping or serving God. I do believe that the problem most people find, as they grow into their faith, is that they were forced to believe everything is handed down through their lineage.

Spirituality

What do you think about when you hear about spirituality? Society tells you that it is related to religion. Society wouldn't be too far off the mark if you had asked me a couple of years ago. My present-day self has a different view of what spirituality is, and Scott echoes my view in their article. Spirituality is tailored to what you believe is in yourself. Your spirit is the driving force behind what you do with your life. Yes, your spirit may be God leading you, but it may also be a version of who or what you believe is guiding you. Could it be the voice of reason? Could it be your conscience? No one, other than you, has those answers. You are in charge of the spirit residing in your soul. Each decision you make has a choice, and you get to control the direction in which your life is going. That is the beauty of being a spiritual person because you know that you get to think and choose for yourself. You don't ever have to be worried about being defined by your spirituality.

Interesting Differences

I thought that it would be appropriate to conclude this sneak peek tour by including a couple of the differences that separate religion and spirituality from each other. I have mentioned that the two are very near and dear to each other, and many people of faith struggle to spot the differences. I do believe that it is important to share the definitions and differences to help individuals understand that they have choices. I struggle to understand the constant tug of war between the two because, at the end of the day, all that is happening is that people are confused about what they are feeling. I want this book to answer all your questions about what is going on in the space around you, and in your mind, body, and soul.

1. Spirituality is tailor-made for each individual; religion is something that you are told you should be experiencing.

2. Spirituality grows with each individual, as they experience life; religion is a prescription that is followed according to the directions of the organization.

3. No one can tell you how to do spirituality—it is a wow moment you come to as you discover and uncover the hidden truths; religion is spoon-fed to a congregation of people who are told what they should be doing according to the gospel.

The third difference is one that I resonate with, and which is why I encourage people from all walks of life to be who they want to be. I also believe that, whether you want to hear it or not, God does love and care for you. Are you ready to join me on this journey? Come on, we have one last piece of business to take care of before we can embark on this spiritual journey.

My Welcome Message to One and All

Stand to attention naysayers, because I have a message to those of you who are reading the Introduction before committing to purchasing this book. I know that you are squinting your eyes to read between the lines. I also know that you are most likely sitting there with your notebook and pen, ready to take notes so that you can leave negative reviews as you "call me out." I would like to tell you that I have been on the other side of the naysayer's fence. I know what you are trying to do because I did it too.

I'm not going to force anyone to do something they are not comfortable with. I want to give you and others a safe space where you will not be stoned, judged, ridiculed, or condemned for your beliefs. You are right where you need to be. Don't judge this book by its cover, the title, or the introduction. Believe and trust in yourself as you slip into comfortable sweats, fluffy socks, find a comfortable place to sit or lie down, and arm yourself with a large bottle of water (and maybe some not-so-healthy snacks). It is not my intention to force you to do something you are not comfortable with. I do believe in giving everyone the freedom of choice. Are you ready to join me on this journey? Yes, I'm asking you, naysayer. Grab my hand as we cross over into the first chapter.

Chapter 1

Defining Your Spirituality

What each of us believes in is up to us, but life is impossible without believing in something. –Kentetsu Takamori

This quote spoke to my soul. I read it standing up, sitting down, tilting my head to the left and right, and even squinting my eyes. It is one of those quotes that doesn't need more than 20 words to send a very clear message. No one knows what struggles you are facing, and no one needs to know because it is something you will share if and when you believe it to be appropriate. I often find myself wondering why adults can't be like children. They are carefree and go through their young lives with so much trust and faith in everyone. It would only be fair to mention that nobody will think twice when a child talks about the magical powers of unicorns. What about their excitement when they "discover" that fairies are living in their gardens, that Santa Claus gave them everything they had on their lists, or that the tooth fairy left a letter, a gift, and some money, under their pillows?

Adults are judged when they proclaim to have an army of angels watching over and protecting them—which in my opinion is more believable. The people I spoke to during my research phase of this book showed me text messages where family or friends are "gently" reminding them that only God can be the protector. Many were ridiculed for their "outlandish" beliefs. I have seen and experienced people's attitudes when I have told them that I believe that angels watch over me. I want to get up close and personal in these people's faces and tell them to read the Bible. Angels are referred to in the

Bible. Oh wait, these people would rather shove the Bible under everyone's noses than know better—right? Okay then, I'll park that here, and allow it to cook while we continue on this journey.

Types of Spirituality

You may be standing at a busy intersection where the traffic lights are not working the way they should. Many approach the intersection carefully. Others may put their faith out there in the universe, floor it, and hope for the best. While some may see the chaotic state from a distance, turn their cars around, and find an alternative route. That is exactly what spirituality is like because something that works for one, may not work for the other. I would like to show you a couple of types of spirituality that may or may not involve religion. Did you know that you are the author of your life? I'll give you a moment for that piece of information to sink in. You are the author, editor, cover designer, content creator, and publisher of your life. You get to add, delete, and modify the path you take in life. The best news of all is that you will take wrong turns, and you will encounter *MANY* questionable choices but you are the best person to right those wrongs.

You need to believe in yourself and listen to that annoying voice in your soul that tries to help you every once in a while. As the author of your life, you get to re-design and finetune all options to suit you. Everything I share can be modified to be beneficial to you. This is not a one-time only deal. Authors write, edit, and re-write portions of their work to remain current. They will remove redundant information that is no longer applicable. You will always be in control, and you always have a choice in which direction your life needs to go.

We have ascertained that spirituality means something different to everyone. You are not here to judge or condemn people for what they believe. You are here to learn what you can do to build up, strengthen, and heal your belief and trust system. You chose to embark on this journey for whatever reasons. I welcomed you with open arms as you stood on the curb, contemplating between entering or running in the other direction. I have reassured you that this is a safe environment where you can be whatever you want, and explore your options to your heart's content.

Spirituality Models

Spirituality is not something you can purchase at the store. It is something that everybody has inside them. Your spirituality may be hiding behind layers of distrust and fear. I have mentioned that you need to have an open and accepting mind to find what you are looking for. I am going to help you peel back the layers, but this is going to be an ongoing process. I am going to share a couple of the models with you. It is important to know that these models are not set in stone, and they are pliable so that you can modify them based on your needs. You are in charge of molding these models because they are important when planning and defining the course of your life.

The Spirit of Intuition

Have you ever had a feeling in the trenches of your stomach that you couldn't put your finger on? You are either unsettled, confused, or intrigued by the feelings you are experiencing. Spiritualists may refer to this model of spirituality as "mystical" because they believe that everything happens for a reason. Many will not agree with the definition of this model because they will have their own beliefs. Guess what? Yes, you know what I'm going to say—it's perfectly fine for them to disagree, and it is not worthy of getting into an argument.

The Spirit of Enlightenment

I will have to admit that this is one of the spiritual models that I have found solace in. I am reminded of when the world was forced to slow down because of a global pandemic that dictated just about every aspect of our lives. I witnessed panic, fear, and uncertainty as I watched people fill up their shopping carts. They were afraid that they would never see the inside of a store again. This is where I started seeing and hearing people for who and what they represented. Many of these people professed to be religious, yet they were the front-runners heading towards nowhere in the "run and panic" race. These were also the people who shared conspiracy theories and bought into the prophecy from the book of Revelations.

I learned a lot about the world and the people in it by focusing on my spiritual model of enlightenment. I adopted a calm demeanor, and I never bought into the panic. I had to stop myself from saying something that would activate a truth bomb among many. Thanks to my spirituality, and the model that I had designed to suit me, I learned to be tolerant and mindful of what others were experiencing. I had to learn that not everyone sees the world the way I do, and that I cannot force people to believe the things I do.

The Spirit of Service

This is another of my favorite spiritual models. I do believe that this one ties in beautifully with the two I have already highlighted. I spoke to someone who is very spiritual and believes that everything they are going through is making them a better person. They believe that every cloud has a silver lining and that things will improve if, and when the time is right. They had experienced hardship because of the global pandemic, but they never spoke about it and continued helping others. Weeks could go by, and they would have no food in their home, but whatever they had, they still shared. One day, the tables were flipped upside down, and this person received the gift of a lifetime—a week's supply of groceries. What followed over the next months (and it still continues as this book is being written), is that the person with the spirit of service continues putting food in their cupboards, and has found someone to do gardening and odd jobs around the house.

The Real Meaning of Spirituality
Being a spiritual person is a private affair. It is not something that should be shouted from the rooftops. I do feel strongly about people looking for a "good job," "you are a great person," or "you will be blessed for all you do." The gift of spirituality doesn't require recognition. Everything you do is part of being selfless. I see the YouTube clips of people doing random acts of kindness, yet, when asked, they will say that they are not doing it for recognition. My question to them is: why are you recording them if you are doing it from the goodness of your heart? I do believe that whatever you do for others will be returned to you. Your deity is not sitting with a score card and tracking all those who are benefiting from your spiritual acts of kindness. Be who you are meant to be, and you will be blessed beyond your wildest dreams.

Believe in Your Faith

No one should be telling you who or what you need to believe in. It is your choice whether you believe in angels, aliens, fairies, or unicorns. If I am outside and being kissed by the sun; I believe that it is the sun pixies dancing around on my skin because their little feet are burning. You may believe that the snowflakes that fall from the sky come from gnomes sitting on the clouds with their ice shavers. The point I am trying to make is that you don't need anyone's approval or acceptance of who or what to believe in. I do believe that you are at the age where you no longer need or require consent to act independently and make decisions for yourself. I am not a dictator, and I am not going to tell you what to do. You get to build your very own personalized pathway that is based on your belief structure.

I do recommend that you put your faith in something or someone you believe in. The title of this section is "Believe in Your Faith" which means that this is about you. It's not about your mom, dad, grandmother, or even the cashier at Costco, and what they think about your choices. You get to explore your spirituality and what is the right fit for you. Will people try to influence you into following their beliefs? Of course, they will, because everyone seems to believe that they will be rewarded for recruiting new "customers." People are always trying to fix something that isn't broken, and that includes who or what you believe in, who you choose to love, or what your bank balance looks like. Most times you just want space and freedom to fall flat on your face when out on a longboard, or learn a valuable life lesson when experiencing a broken heart.

I love the idea of being in control of my beliefs and spirituality because I am the one who is responsible for the choices I make; regardless of the consequences. The reflection looking back at me in the mirror tells me that I am a unique individual. You don't go to school to learn about pleasing people you interact with. You grow up being told about God, Jesus, Allah, or Buddha, as well as angels, tooth fairies, or mermaids. Some may have been forced to attend church and Sunday schools, or to sit in the temple and observe. I have finally reached the stage of my life where I know that I found something that is tailor-made for me. I want to help you find your unique fit, one that will make you feel that you have a purpose. I believe that your spirituality will find you, and when it does, you will know it. That is when your spirit will light up and your purpose will be revealed.

Spiritual Practices

I may have mentioned, or at the very least implied, that I will use whatever I feel is necessary to build, mold, and strengthen my spirituality so that I can benefit. You don't have to be religious to have faith, and you don't need to be religious or spiritual to have a belief system in place. Everything I am sharing can be used together or as standalone tools or practice. I have said this before and I will more than likely say it a couple more times, but you don't have to follow anyone's lead. You get to be you, by choosing what fits in with your lifestyle and is executed by you.

The tools I will be listing are ones you have heard of before. They are not limited, and you have the freedom to use whatever speaks to your soul. These tools are going to help you block all the negativity, condemnation, and judgmental noise that causes a haze of feeling unworthy, insecure, and angry. Your little place under the sun will bring you joy, love, peace, and more butterflies than you have ever seen. This is where you will experience the healing your soul needs, and where you can return to multiple times a day to recharge your spiritual energy. Let's take a look at a list of practices you can participate in to bring your soul—happiness.

- Meditation; guided or focused.
- Prayer; a conversation with whomever you believe in.
- Breathing techniques to connect with your soul.
- Exercise such as yoga or Pilates.
- Daily affirmations, mantras, and chanting.

The spiritual practices I have shared are only ideas of what you can do to build up and strengthen your spirituality. I have been where you most likely are. I sat on the outside of the spiritual bubble. My faith, spirituality, and beliefs went into hiding because I was being peppered with judgment and bullying. I refused to conform to what everyone was telling or expecting of me. I had built up resentment towards those who would tell me my life is doomed because I have fallen off the path. Do I believe that I have fallen off the path? Do I believe that my life is doomed? No, because I am the person I was meant to be. I don't need to live in a fishbowl and put myself on display for everyone to tap on the glass to get a reaction out of me. The most wonderful experience I had from the healing practices that I adopted into my daily life, was that I was in control of the remote to block everyone out. I would just like to say that the remote is one of the most hated and "evil" spiritual tools I have ever come across. The people who dare to judge or bully me for my beliefs have tried to take them away from me because they know that I will not step down for them.

The Spiritual Journey Continues

It is time to move on and uncover a chest full of spiritual treasures that will help you design the life you want. What you have learned in this chapter has been a droplet in comparison to everything you are going to leave with. I am looking forward to continuing this journey with you. Together we will learn about the composition of our spirits. We will also learn how to become friends with our perfect imperfections. The future may look bleak and blurry at present; especially as we feel our way through the uncertainty. I know, without a shadow of a doubt, that the view will become crystal clear. All we need to do is have hope, faith, and belief that we are in control of our future. We can't predict what tomorrow will bring to the table, but from where I'm sitting, today isn't looking too bad. Come along, and let's move on to the next chapter.

Chapter 2
It's All About Your Hidden Inner Treasure Trove

I have found that people are quick to judge others based on their physical features, or lack thereof. It wouldn't be presumptuous to agree that everyone has passed some or other type of comment referring to the way someone looks, acts, or thinks. We could pass it off as us being in a mood or chalk it up as being a jealous person. No one—not you, me, nor the elements of the earth—knows what someone is going through. This is where the *Spirit of Enlightenment* takes possession of all your common senses and forces you to see everyone through clear lenses. It is, unfortunately, human nature to judge that book by its cover because we don't know how to compartmentalize the vision before us.

The change that we envision has to come from each individual that walks on this earth. We all have to learn how to like, love, and accept ourselves before we can appreciate the beauty of what everyone else has to offer. It is a tall order for many because what we believe may not align with what someone else represents. Every person that walks on this earth is special and unique, and has many hidden attributes that they are afraid to share. Many may not be aware of what they are capable of doing. You may walk past someone and smile without thinking about it too much. You may not be aware that the person you walked by needed to see your smile because they are going through something difficult. You don't think about what your actions may mean to family, friends, or strangers.

I want to use this book as a means to show you how special and unique you are. You may believe that you have nothing of significance to offer others. I am going to shake your tree and tell you that you—yes *YOU*—have more to share with others than you will ever know. I am going to shake the thicket you are hiding in, and help you navigate your way to the clearing where you will see in yourself, what others see in you. This is not about who dresses the best, who has the most resources, or who is better at diffusing a volatile situation. This is all about unlocking what your mind has been reluctant to believe and understand. It is time to realize your true worth by understanding how your mind works.

Exploring Your Inner Jungle

- Why is it so difficult for you to believe that you are a good person with good intentions?

- What has happened to make you believe that you don't deserve happiness?

- Why have you allowed society to categorize you based on their beliefs and ideals?

These are pretty hard questions to answer because we don't have the answers. These are the types of questions that will have roughly three and a half billion different answers. Each of these answers is hidden between the leaves of the jungle within our souls. I have come up with a plan of action, which I believe will work for everyone who is looking for answers as they explore their spirituality. We are going to search for that elusive trove of artifacts that have been hidden. The lessons learned are going to help you find the peace of mind you have been yearning for. You are going to learn how to identify the best part of you that has been hidden. Are you ready to clear your spiritual jungle and explore the hidden passages of your mind?

Understanding the Value of Your Treasure Trove

What is so special about this elusive treasure trove? What value does it add to your life? I believe that everyone has been given a gift on the day that they are born into this world. The gifts will change as we grow and experience life. You will become more guarded the older you become. You will experience hardships, failures, and disappointment—but you will also experience happiness, love, and freedom. I will say it again that no two people will have the same experience. Many people will stand up, dust themselves off, and continue living their lives; while others will be too afraid to pick themselves up to start over. They will ignore the calling in their souls to share the treasures in their troves with others. Some may blame society for setting a precedent that allows for bullying, condemnation, and ridicule. We see it in the way youngsters speak and treat people who are older than them. We witness body shaming when clothing companies promote their products.

I often find myself wondering why people would find it necessary to be mean or pass negative comments about people they don't know. I have witnessed smear campaigns against successful social media influencers who are subjected to snide comments when they do shopping hauls or go on vacations. I have interviewees who have shared about members of their community who have no regard for people's feelings, and they will belittle them and make their victims feel as if they are at fault. One of these abusers is a 94-year-old who inserts themselves into everyone's business, will start an argument, and when that argument doesn't work in their favor—will cry wolf. I remember looking at the evidence receipts, and my jaw dropped. These people who thrive on confrontation, condemnation, judgment, and all things negative are responsible for burying others' treasure chests under layers of fear and uncertainty.

You may be curious to find out what is in these treasure chests I keep referring to. Let's take a stroll through the treasure troves department to see what we may find. Another one of my gentle reminders needs to be inserted here to remind us all that not everyone will have the same treasures. You are also reminded that you may be utilizing the items in your treasure chest without realizing it, and whatever you uncover may come as a very pleasant surprise to you.

Identifying Your Treasures

Many people have the treasure of being the gift of the givers. These types of people are hard workers and successful at what they do. They will use their resources to help others or build up their communities. I am reminded of the social media influencers who are ridiculed for their shopping hauls and going on destination vacations. No one knows what these people do behind the scenes to share their wealth. Who are we to judge what people are doing with the money they have earned promoting and sharing themselves online? What happens if we were to flip the tables and take the social media influencers out of the equation, and put them in a working-class scenario—would shopping hauls and vacations be ridiculed?

Other types of treasures include caring souls who go above and beyond the call of duty to help people. These caring souls could be nurses, teachers, or regular people who bless others who need a smile, a plate of warm food, or a break from whatever they are going through. These are all people who do good and don't look for recognition. They are using their treasures to spread kindness, caring, and yes, maybe some financial reprieve. No one can tell you what you will find when you open the lid to your treasure chest. Each person will find something that is unique to them and their calling in life. I have said it before, and I will say it again; keep an open mind at all times. Clear away the obstacles, such as self-doubt and negativity. Embrace the gifts that peek at you from the treasure chest. Give those gifts a chance to work some magic in your life, and in the lives of those you are going to be touching.

Dispersing Your Treasures

Sharing is caring is an idiom that I was introduced to at a very young age. I recall my kindergarten teacher saying it to children who wouldn't share something that was meant for the whole class, such as puzzles, coloring pencils, or toys. This was one of the first lessons you are taught as a child. Many have lost their ability to share for some or other reason. They may have learned what it was like to have and hold onto something that others wanted because they didn't want to share. One of my interviewees told me that they would never be wealthy because they are always sharing or giving away things to help others. When I queried their reasoning for sharing or giving things away; they told me that they want to see smiles. I asked them if there was a possibility that the items that were gifted with a good heart—were being sold for profit, and they told me that they had told the beneficiary that they would prefer that they didn't sell it for monetary gain. They continued to tell me that it is a matter of trust, and you can't change the way others think or act.

Sharing your wealth does not refer to material or financial treasures. I am a firm believer that our spirits or souls have an unlimited supply of gifts that are waiting to be shared with family, friends, and strangers. That unlimited supply of gifts is not defined by what you possess but by what you have may have that will help others grow from strength to strength. Let's take a look at some of the treasures that you may have hidden between the layers of your spiritual jungle that you didn't know existed. Sharing what is in your treasure chests is a way for you to mold your spiritual model. Now, no one is telling you to share everything you possess—unless it is something your spirit is imprinting on your soul. Sharing is meant to be a selfless act. Sharing your spiritual treasures is not meant to be done for personal gain, or recognition and praise. Let's take a look at some of the different types of spiritual treasures that you can disperse among members of your immediate circle, or your community.

- Find employment or a volunteer organization where your talents are appreciated.

- Being a motivational speaker by sharing your spiritual journey and helping others realize their treasure troves.

- Use your spiritual gifts to speak out about what matters that you believe in.

Everything that I have shared is a full-circle cycle that incorporates your feelings. I do believe that your treasure trove speaks to you and what is hidden within you. The talents and gifts that are mentioned, and will most likely be mentioned going forward, are unique to you. Some people may find that their talent is writing, while others will find that they are better at being vocal. Some may be musicians who can make magic with any musical instrument, while others have the voices of angels. You have to find something that you are good at, and don't allow outside influences to dictate what they believe your talents to be. Go with your heart, and listen to your gut intuition.

Connecting Your Mind to Your Inner Treasure

No matter where you are in your life's journey, you have an obligation to yourself to be kind, courteous, and understanding to the most important person in your life—*YOU!* It cannot be stressed enough how important you are to the world. You may roll your eyes. You may shake your head in denial. You may even tear up because someone has always told you that you are a disappointment. I want you to know—from a spiritual person's point of view—that you are loved. You were loved from the moment you were placed in your parent's arms. You were brought to this earth with a purpose and a destiny in mind. No one knows what their destinies are, and we go through life doing whatever we want until we notice a balance shift.

You are not perfect. I am not perfect. We are perfect imperfections that have yet to find our purpose. I love using that analogy because no two people have the same scars, blemishes, or fingerprints. I recently heard a talk where the speaker said that people spend so much time following directions from "perfect" people that they cannot appreciate the reflection looking back at them. Society is to blame for this because of the idea that we need to fit in a box with very specific dimensions, and if we don't comply with those specifications, we become outcasts. This is the type of attitude that covers our treasure chests and hides them behind thickets so that they cannot be found. We fear our treasure chests because we are afraid of what others think of us. What we are doing is playing into the hands of those who want to limit and suppress the treasures everyone has to offer the world.

Breaking the Molds of Negativity

Are you aware of the restrictions involved with being in a negative environment, or being in the company of a person who cannot see good in anyone or anything? I can relate to my experience which found me struggling to breathe, I felt anxious and depressed, my energy was depleted the moment I entered that situation, and I was just generally feeling unwell. I clawed my way out of that tunnel, and when I found the light again, I vowed never to return to that dark space. I know, and understand, that it may not be easy to leave that negative situation because you may be burdened by the baggage that is packed onto your shoulders.

It is my wish, that everyone who finds themselves in a situation where they are trapped and held hostage by negativity which includes condemnation, judgment, and ridicule, can find a way to walk away from the situation unscathed. I have a sliver of hope for those who want to leave their negative situation. You may just aim your water bottle at me because yes, I am going to tell you to start working on your positives. This is something that we will be discussing further in the book, but for now, it is important for you to think about positivity, believe that it can happen, and know that it is an achievable goal. Those are the most important ingredients to help you find your light, and in doing so, you will discover your inner treasure chest.

- Is it possible to find healing by being positive?
- Do you have what it takes to spread positivity?
- Are you ready to conquer the world (or your community) with your newfound positivity?
- Can you be the voice of reason when deciding between right and wrong?
- Will you be the person who will help those who are struggling to find the right path on their journey through life?

If you can ask and answer any questions that refer to life lessons, those less fortunate than yourself or share your stories with others; you have what it takes to spread positivity. You may think that you have nothing, which we have previously mentioned, but your smile may just have saved the life of someone who was about to do something that would hurt themselves, or their families. You may not think very much about your smile, but I can assure you that a smile—whether crooked, straight, thin-lipped, or dry and flaky—reaches the eyes. I have been told that the eyes are the windows to the soul. I do believe we have come full circle because this book is all about what your soul and spirit can do for yourself, and others.

Let's go straight into the next chapter, where we are going to continue learning about your mind, positivity, and how you can become a better, more refined version of the person you deserve to be.

Chapter 3

Altering the Way You Think

- Have you allowed changes to slip through your fingers because you thought about it but never did anything?

- Have you watched someone else get praise and recognition for one of your ideas?

- Are you afraid of change?

I was recently reminded that changes don't happen on their own. Change is something that each one of us has within our souls. We all have choices, as previously discussed, yet we are afraid to choose because we are afraid. You may be tapping your foot, shaking your head, or breathing heavily as you become agitated at my statements and questions. Stop for a moment, and think about what I have said. What is holding you back? Is it the fear of judgment? Could it be that you don't believe in yourself? Maybe you don't want to be the one who will be labeled as a failure if your idea doesn't work. I can assure you that everyone who is reading this has been sitting on the same fence where you currently find yourself. I do believe that it is safe to say that everyone sitting or standing near that fence, is being covered by the umbrella of fear of intimidation.

I want you to know that this book is not about regrets or missed opportunities. You are not going to be pointing any fingers at yourself or anyone else. A large part of the process of being positive—is accepting that you can't change something that has happened. There is no way for you to go back to the past to alter something that will benefit your future. What happened cannot be undone, but you can learn from the past to make today good, and ensure that tomorrow will be near perfect. The past is exactly where it belongs—in the graveyards of yesterday. You can spend your time looking for the silver linings around the dark clouds, but then you are wasting precious time. Ask yourself why you are here. Always be honest with yourself, because this is your journey and you don't have to answer anyone. You are adult enough to hold yourself accountable for the direction in which your life is going.

You are here because you want to reconnect with your spirit and soul. You want to strengthen your hope, trust, belief, and faith in yourself. You want to learn how to strengthen your mind, body, and soul so that you can share your inner treasures with those around you. Everything you want to learn and gain from this book is in the palm of your hands. You have to overcome a very important obstacle before you can achieve that smooth journey to your spiritual oasis. You are going to continue where you left off in Chapter 2, and that is learning how to unlock your mind palace that you have been protecting.

Opening the Doors to Your Mind Palace

The world is a busy place. The people in this busy world are diverse. The universe is divided into continents, countries, cities, towns, villages, and so many more nooks and crooks. Each one of these continents, countries, cities, or towns is inhabited by people. Each of these places has rules and laws that inhabitants have to abide by to be on the right side of the law. We know that it is human nature to find loopholes in existing rules and regulations. Some people may even decide that they are above the rules and go and do whatever they want which includes theft, intentionally hurting others, doing questionable things, and murder. Many may argue that they didn't know what they were doing or that they were possessed by some or other demonic entity. I am not here to pass judgments on what other people may or may not be going through.

I am here to nudge you—whether gently or by force—to pick open the doors to your mind palace. You are going to learn how to unlock, unblock, and realize that what you have hidden behind the lock and key has a place in this busy world you are a part of. You don't have to be afraid to listen to the voices in your head. All mind restrictions and mandates have been sent to a place where you no longer have to be part. This is where I get to tell you that you are allowed to be a free thinker. You are allowed to have an opinion that relates to you and the journey you are on. You don't need to hide behind the filter of fear any longer. The road to discovering your spirituality doesn't have to be a lonely one. Each journey has to start somewhere, and an excellent starting point is recognizing you are in control of your mind palace.

This chapter is all about helping you open the doors that you have locked and sealed. The journey to your spiritual oasis needs to go through the spring-cleaning process where you open up and air out all the rooms. The cleaning process includes clearing cobwebs, attacking the dust bunnies, and inspecting the garbage that had been swept under the rugs. Yes, I did say rugs because your mind palace is a very large place that holds more information, knowledge, happiness, pain, anger, and ideas than any library you have ever seen. No one ever said, or will agree, that cleaning is an easy process. Thankfully you won't need harmful chemicals or expensive gadgets to clean your mind palace. Everything you need is right before you and easily accessible. Come one, let's go and access the rooms you have had locked and sealed. It's time to remove the doors from the hinges, and open all the windows. We are about to retrain your mind into trusting your soul and being who you are meant to be.

It's All in the Planning: Altering the Way You Think

STOP! Don't reach for the panic paddles just yet. This chapter is not about me attempting to enter your mind and perform mind control techniques. You will not be clucking around like a chicken, nor will you be doing something untoward. You can sit back, release a sigh of relief, and relax knowing that I am not your enemy. Everything I am doing in this book is based on my passion in life; which is to help people realize that they are important and that they can make a difference. The twists, turns, and obstacles are necessary to help you find your spiritual oasis. You have to learn to find, identify, and listen to your voice. You have an obligation to yourself, to believe in whatever you have to share or offer to those around you. Remember that your spiritual models are created by the special gifts and talents that you have in your inner treasure chest. I don't need to remind you that your spiritual models need clear directions on the route on which you are embarking. You are the engineer, designer, and author of this transformation process, and all changes begin and end with you.

This is the part where everyone wants to dive in head first. I can tell you that you won't find any fast passes in this book. A large part of my process is to promote a slow and steady pace. Everyone will reach the finish line at some stage during their journey. Some may take a little longer than others to get there, but it's one of those journeys where you gain life experience along the way. You are going to learn to take your time, and enjoy the process that it takes to get you where you are going. Patience is another wonderful little addition to your toolkit; it will come in handy. Let's take a look at a list of steps you can implement to sort through the dredges of your mind palace.

- Envision the changes you want in your life.

- Knock guilt out of the park, and be proud of who and what you are.

- Distance yourself from negativity.

- Empower yourself with all things positive.

- Yesterday has reached its expiration date, and tomorrow is yet to present itself, but today is here, ready and waiting for you to do everything that you didn't do yesterday and what you may need to do tomorrow.

- It's okay to dream about the direction in which your spiritual gifts should go; it is part of another little tool I like to call manifesting.

- Think about everything that is presenting you with an obstacle that is stopping you from reaching your potential.

- Have multiple plans for when your original plan doesn't go according to plan, or if the directives change—don't settle for second best.

- Journaling—drawing the words, feelings, and emotions out of your mind needs a safe resting place.

- Don't be afraid to ask for something you want or need—manifest your needs and wants, and try until you are successful.

- Break the cycle of questioning how you will do something, and start believing that you can do anything you put your mind to.

- Self-appreciation is another tool that will help you on your spiritual journey; surround yourself with positive affirmations and soak up all the motivation from those who support your journey.

Redecorating Your Mind Palace

The list I shared in the previous section forms part of the blueprints of your mind palace. Remember that this is about you, and you don't have to feel guilty about choosing yourself over someone else. Your mind, body, and soul rely on your overall health and wellbeing to be in tip-top shape so that your spiritual oasis can flourish and overflow with all the riches you have to share.

The next time someone tells you that you are selfish or that you don't care about their unimportant woes—which you will know whether they are in the middle of a real "crisis"—remind them that you need to take care of yourself before you can take care of them. I have found that this method gives the other party time to think, it teaches them to have patience, and understand that their priorities may not be as important as they believe. In short, everyone has time to assess the situation.

We all have people in our lives who demand our immediate attention. Family, friends, educators, acquaintances, or colleagues may not understand that "wait" is a word that applies to them. This is an intimidation tactic that I have seen in practice by many. The person on the other side of that guilt line is afraid to challenge the situation, because they have most likely been burned once, twice, or many times. I am going to sound like a broken record getting stuck on a deep scratch, but you have the right to say no and walk away. You have to do what makes you happy. Guess what? You are in control, and these demanding individuals have no legs to stand on because you have what they want, and they won't get it until you are ready.

Decide what you want, set your terms and conditions in writing, and follow through (don't back down). Those are three more tools that you can add to your toolkit as you continue along with this journey of finding your spiritual oasis. Let's take a look at some helpful steps you may want to add to your backpack as we look at ways to nudge you and your powerful mind, onto the path that will lead you to your spiritual oasis.

Journaling

Some may see this practice of journaling as nothing but a teenage girl's escape room. I would hate to be the one to pop that bubble, but I'm going to obliterate that idea. Journaling is something everyone—regardless of age, gender, ethnicity, or religion—can practice. There is nothing better than drawing positive, negative, happy, or fearful words and emotions from the deepest trenches of your soul and putting them on paper. The exercise of journaling is an effective tool for cleaning your mind palace. Keeping track of your daily thoughts will help you form a pattern that may be beneficial to your spiritual journey.

Positive Affirmations and Motivational Pep Talks

Have you ever talked to yourself? Have you ever caught someone looking at you as you talk to yourself? There is no shame in admitting that you are one or both of these types of people. Who is anyone to judge someone who is talking to the voices in their heads? This may be an unpopular belief, but I believe that the voices are real. They hold us accountable when we do something wrong. They will nag us, just like our parents, to do the right thing. They will stop at nothing to make us give them some attention. Do you still want to tell me that those voices in your head are on a train destined for the asylum?

Two can play the game—you and the voices in your head. This is where you come in with your positive affirmations. This is a really neat game but you will need scraps of paper or sticky notes. Next, you are going to write down everything that you love about yourself.

This is all about positivity, and I can promise you that negative images of yourself will not be tolerated. The next stage of this game is to walk around your home and put the notes in all the places you will see them such as on mirrors, on the closet doors, or on the refrigerator. Read these notes multiple times a day, as you walk, and believe what you are reading about yourself. At the end of each day, focus on one of the affirmations and give yourself a motivational pep talk. I do believe that the more times you raise yourself, the more you will believe that you can overcome major obstacles in life.

Lower the Bar of Expectation

You shouldn't frown so much because you will get lines on your face, and find it necessary to go for Botox treatment. I do acknowledge that this chapter is about reprogramming the way your mind works so that you can release your inner treasures. I am not bringing negativity in here, but I am cautioning you to always be prepared for the unexpected. Life has a funny way of kicking you in the shins when you least expect it. When that happens, you are most likely going to feel as if you are at fault, blame yourself, regress, and close the newly opened doors quicker than it took to read the introduction of this book. Always allow wiggle room for things to go wrong or not work out according to your plotting and planning. You have nothing to be ashamed of if something doesn't work the way you envisioned. Stop being your worst enemy. Pull up your big people's socks, slip on the Crocs, and hit the reset button.

Furnishing Your Mind Palace

I would like to remind you that the process of spring cleaning your mind palace is not a task that can or should be rushed. Finding yourself between the debris is a healing process that needs time. I gave you some points under the sub-heading of *It's All in the Planning: Altering the Way You Think*. Those points can be used to aid your healing process and unlock chambers in your mind palace that you had forgotten. I touched on a couple in the following section, to give you an indication of how they are geared towards you. As I have previously mentioned, everything I have mentioned in the list can be customized to suit your situation. I hope that you have found this chapter as healing as it was intended. Healing your mind is one small step on the journey to your spiritual oasis.

Are you ready for some decorating tips? You won't need paint and power tools for this re-model. The next leg of this journey is going to be about furnishing your mind palace. I'm not talking about lavish room makeovers with new beds, swinging chandeliers, arcade machine games, and three closets filled with name-branded clothing and shoes. This room makeover is going to be filled with your dreams. Your dreams are going to be taken into account, and you are going to learn how to manifest these dreams. Let's get hopping.

Chapter 4

Don't Be Afraid to Reach for Your Dreams

Love what you do and do what you love. Don't listen to anyone else who tells you not to do it. You do what you want, what you love. Imagination should be the center of your life. –Ray Bradbury

- Would you give up on a dream because someone may not share your passion or vision?

- Do you believe that you are feeding the insecurities of those who ridicule those who dare to dream?

- Are you ready to reach for your dreams without fear?

Dreams are fantasies about what you would like to achieve in your lifetime. Everyone has or had one or many dreams. Many have worked hard to achieve their dreams and walked through treacherous terrain to make their dreams a reality. Others have been afraid to share their dreams because of insecurities, and have shoved them into boxes and stored them in their mind palaces.

This book has taken you on a rollercoaster ride that is quite a way from being over. I have had you exploring your innermost treasure chests which had been buried beneath debris. We have done a spring clean to clear your mind palace, and find and execute the tools needed to help you improve the way you think. All this has been done with one huge goal in sight—which is to find your spiritual oasis. The cleansing process is far from over, and you have a way to go. Realizing your dreams is just another one of the chambers within your mind palace that have created an obstacle on your journey to your spiritual oasis.

This chapter is about me or anyone giving you permission or the go-ahead to dream. This chapter is about gently nudging you through the obstacles that are preventing you from moving forward. You are in control of every part of you, and that includes your thoughts and the choices you make. The cleaning process also gives you the upper hand when it comes to taking action against the vagrants who are freeloading in your mind palace. You hold all the cleaning tools, which include and are not limited to brooms, mops, vacuum cleaners, steam cleaners, sanitizers, and everything that is needed for a thorough deep clean.

Becoming Part of the Dream Team—Again

Let's assume you were once part of the "Dream Team." You had dreams, and possibly even a vision board that had a five-or-ten-year plan to make those dreams a reality. Something may have happened that crushed any hopes of your dreams from seeing the light. Alternatively, someone could have commented on your carefully thought out and planned dreams to burst all the bubbles you had created. We can't speak or think for others, and we will never understand why someone would rob us of our dreams. They are your dreams, and they don't affect anyone around you. I do believe that each person should be held accountable for the dreams that are hidden in the chambers of the mind palace. Hear me out before you start tapping your foot and your nostrils start flaring.

This journey that you have embarked on is about healing and finding your place in this crazy world. You want to find out where you fit in, which is an excellent move because we all know that everyone has an opinion about everything. I have repeatedly told you that you have the freedom of choice, and you are entitled to make decisions based on what suits you. I know and understand that you may be afraid of standing up to people, especially close family and friends who want you to fit into their glass jars. It is okay to want to fit into a glass jar of your choice. You shouldn't have to be afraid to do what you want to do and achieve the results you have dreamed of.

Someone told me that they had lived their life making everyone, from family and friends–to the tellers at the store and the dry cleaner, happy. They would assist the tellers at the store because they didn't want to give them more work than necessary. The dry cleaner would smile broadly because they knew that they would be saving on cleaning products. Family and friends took advantage of them because they were always willing to stop what they were doing to help them.

That is how dreams become dust collectors in the secret chambers of mind palaces. Now, I do agree—to some extent—that everyone is accountable for their dreams and the direction in which they go. We're not going to wallow in "what ifs" because as you have learned—you can't change the past. You may agree that the cleansing process you are currently participating in is allowing you to wipe the slate clean. Take a look at, and reassess your dusty dreams that have been hiding in the secret chamber. Revive the dreams if they are still relevant, remove those that have sailed into the sunset, or create brand new dreams. It is time to get rid of the dust bunnies and take a look at ways in which you can realize your dreams.

Setting Your Dream Goals

The dream chamber has been opened. The dust bunnies have been banished for the time being. The spring-cleaning process is in full swing. The first, and most important step on your to-do list, is to have goals in place. Goals are an important tool in all life situations because they teach you about accountability. Having goals in place will help you prepare for any unexpected obstacles that are aimed at changing the course of your journey through life. Obstacles present themselves in many different ways which include fear, procrastination, or negativity from family, friends, or colleagues. You are once again reminded that this journey to your spiritual oasis is a bumpy road filled with ridicule, condemnation, or judgment. It is your duty to navigate your way through those obstacles, and not allow them to deter you from where you want to be.

You may want to grab your journal for the next part. I am going to share a list that you have to answer honestly. The list will guide you to set up foolproof dream goals. Remember that all dream goals are determined by what you want to see happen in your future. You hold your dreams in the palm of your hand, and you are the only one who can change the outcome. I would recommend that you allocate each dream with its own set of goals. This helps you stay on the right path, and yes, holds you accountable.

- Think about what you want; is it a success, is it to build a house, is it to travel around the world, or is it to write a book?

- Think about why you want this dream to be successful.

- Envision the end result; ask yourself if you will need help reaching your dream goals, or if you can reach them on your own.

- Achievability plays an important role when setting goals, so you may want to assess whether you will follow through or give up when you don't achieve the desired outcome.

- The most important step of this list is to determine a timeline for your dream to become a reality; be reasonable, and take your time getting there.

I have to add that each of these points can be re-assessed to suit wherever you are in your journey through life. Goals do change, and again, it is not a sign of weakness to alter them but don't give up on your dreams. You can have two types of goals; one being long term as pointed out above. You could also have per week or per month short-term goals that will help you reach those long-term goals. Don't allow your fears to snuff the life out of your dreams.

The Dream Menu of Success

You should be proud of yourself. You have accomplished a couple of mammoth tasks on this journey to your spiritual oasis. You can add checkmarks next to the tasks that you have accomplished:

- opening the dream chamber in your mind palace
- re-allocating the dust bunnies
- sorting through, getting rid of, or reviving redundant dreams
- setting achievable goals

When you take a look at all that you have accomplished in this chapter, you should be proud of yourself. You have stepped out of the dark corner where you have been hiding because of fear. I have expressed that you have nothing to be afraid of. I know and understand that words hurt, but you have it in you to show those who continually want to crush you, that you are stronger. Be as selfish as you need to be to find yourself.

The "Dream Menu of Success" is designed for people like you—who stop, drop, and roll when someone demands attention. This menu is not a standard menu where you can order something and it will be delivered. This is a menu that you can implement in your daily life to help you realize your dreams. Tweak the menu, and do what needs to be done, but don't neglect yourself and your dreams. Let's do a whole lot of manifesting to get this menu to do the task it is meant to accomplish.

Visualize Your Dream Becoming a Reality

There is no such thing as a dream that is too big or too small. All dreams are a perfect size. Another approach that might help you see your vision a little clearer is imagining all the little dreams fitting together to become a big dream. There is nothing wrong with dreaming about something you want. We're not going to pretend that everyone is going to agree with the dreams you have, and that is perfectly fine. Remember that you are not here to satisfy everyone because you are the most important person on this journey.

Go ahead and visualize your dream becoming a reality. Keep your chin up, remain positive, and strive toward grabbing the prize at the end of the dream. I would like to arm you with a couple of mantras that you can use going forward. It is also a way for you to strengthen your positivity and keep you focused.

- I am allowed to dream.
- I will dream as big or as small as I want.
- I can dream about anything.
- My dream will come true.

You are going to start working on removing all negative hints such as "maybe I will," "it will never work," or "I can't do it." Did you know that the use of positive affirmations becomes a habit that is healing for your mind, body, and soul? You have to keep saying it for you to believe it.

You Don't Have to Do It All Today

Everybody goes through periods where their dreams seem unattainable. You may wake up in the morning and just not "feel" like today is a good day. You may want to stay in pajamas, sit on the couch with a bucket of popcorn, and binge-watch a series. Did you know that everyone is allowed to have time off to do nothing but be a couch potato? You didn't? Well, now you know. The most important takeaway is that you do not give up. It's okay if yesterday was a difficult day, and you head-butted a couple of people who weren't interested in allowing you to focus on your dream. We all fall into that rutted groove where the soul feels defeated, and you want to throw all the towels in the ring, but you remind yourself that you are the CEO of your dream chamber. I'm going to give you a couple of tips to help you out of your rutted groove. You will be back in your dream chamber, where you can re-assess your goals, and put one toe in front of the other until you are ready to run your marathon again.

- Spend some time journaling your thoughts and emotions.
- Exercise; grab your vacuum cleaner, turn the music up, and dance as you kill a couple of birds with one stone.
- Spend time meditating and practicing breathing techniques.
- Ensure you get enough rest.

The Highway to Manifesting Your Dreams

It is good to have dreams. It is even better to have goals that will turn dreams into reality. It would be even better if everyone supported your "dare to dream big" campaign. It is disheartening when the people you love, look up to, and trust don't share your excitement. You feel defeated and broken because you believed that the dream you have for your future is attainable, and will benefit everyone in your life. I am here to lift you up, grab you by the shoulders, and tell you that you are the most important person on this journey. Continue dreaming your dreams; don't ever allow anyone to rob you of the items in your mind palace.

I want you to keep your list of goals close as we continue on to the next chapter. I have a sneaky feeling that you may just be modifying your goals as we dive into the chapter that I have been hinting at—manifesting your intentions. Are you ready to jump into the next chapter? Come on, let's go.

Chapter 5
All Things are Possible—The Power of Manifesting Your Dreams and Desires

The Law of Attraction states that whatever you focus on, think about, read about, and talk about intensely, you're going to attract more of it into your life.
–Jack Canfield

I am an eternal optimist who believes that everything happens according to the plans the universe has for the day. Not many people will agree with my optimism and will find ways to prove that my beliefs have no place in this world. Yes, I have been there, done that, and burned the t-shirt a couple of times. The way I see it—I am part of this world for a reason. I may not know why I am here, or what I need to do, but I believe that all plans will be revealed when the time is right. Until such time, I see it as my duty to do good by being positive, being of service to others, and realizing my dreams.

I have been sowing the seeds of manifestation since Chapter 3. I know that sending your dreams, desires, and intentions out into the universe is not something everyone believes in. It is like being a toddler and visiting Santa Clause at the mall. You would sit on his lap or stand beside him to share your Christmas wish list. You believed that you would be getting the game, the Barbie, the football, or the book that you desperately wanted. Christmas morning would come, and you would get everything you asked for, and more. The older you got—you began to realize that Santa Clause was just one of the millions of sweaty people in red costumes with oversized pillows as their bellies. The point of this little visual is to help you understand that in your childhood years, you believed in manifesting your dreams and desires, and got what you hoped for.

Adults have a hard time understanding this shift and will argue that children don't know the difference between fact and fiction. I can tell you, from experience, that adults had a tough time distinguishing between the two as well. This chapter is a special one for me because I am always looking for ways to help others who need some "good vibrations" after a tough couple of years where a global pandemic, as well as death and destruction, has dominated the media headlines. I'm not saying that you should go out into the world and fight some battles that may or may not claim your life, but I am implying that the universe could do with an outpouring of positive energy from you. It only takes one person to start a trend—you can be the one person.

It's About What You Can Do for the Universe

I have previously mentioned that you are special and that you are on this earth for a reason. I am pretty sure I detected a couple of raised eyebrows, and many frowns when I mentioned it. And yes, we're a couple of chapters in, and I do still believe that everyone on this earth is here for a purpose. I have spoken to many people while doing research for this book because I am curious about what others are doing, how they cope with whatever is weighing them down, and the plans they have for their lives. I spoke to a diverse group of people and the responses have been varied.

- Some people go through life expecting everything to be handed to them on a silver platter.

- Some people don't believe that they add value to their communities, the world, or the people they meet.

- Some people wanted to hit me with their bibles.

- Some people have adopted various spiritual models in their lives, which have led them to want to give back to the universe.

- Some people believe that you get back what you give.

This is what makes the world we live in so unique. There happens to be more than enough space for everyone. Some people may want to argue that this earth is too small and that everyone needs to jump onto the same page. Someone asked me a question many years ago, and I ask myself numerous times a day—especially when I see comments that should have remained in that individual's mind palace—"can you imagine living in a world where everyone dressed, walked, and spoke the same?" The thought of being a carbon copy of everyone else doesn't sit well with me. I love that we are diverse. I would love it even more if everyone in the world got along, but that is a tall order and one we can throw out into the universe so that I can manifest my desires and dreams.

That is why this chapter is so special to me. You don't need to look a certain way, be a specific body type, follow a specific religion, or have a line of credit that spins around the world a couple of times. I cannot stress it enough that you are part of this world because you add something that is needed. We may not know what special spice you add to this world, but someone higher than you, me, and the entire human race hold all the answers. That is what manifesting is all about, and now I get to guide you through the laws of attraction, which is an extended addendum of manifestation.

Clarity Through Contrast: Getting the Results You Desire

I had to return to this section of the chapter when I reached the end because something didn't feel right. I wouldn't be surprised if it was the universe telling me that I was missing an important step in stressing manifestation while missing the importance of clarity via contrast. Even writers miss the flags when they are excited about a topic that has brought them to where they are sharing their hearts and souls with strangers. We just want to share everything that we can squeeze in without overwhelming everyone with their thoughts, opinions, and ideas.

The clarity through contrast technique is based on the goals you have set up for yourself. I would like to share a list of techniques that you could implement into your dream menu when setting new goals or modifying existing ones. You need to believe in your goals, and you need to approach with an attitude that elevates your intention to follow through, implement them, and believe in what you are doing. Don't hold back on your visions because you don't believe in your ability to be successful. You will never know what will happen if you don't take a giant leap of faith. You can't expect something to happen if you sit back with your legs up on the table in front of you with your arms crossed behind your head. Dare to dream, and dare to believe that something good will happen. Honestly, what do you have to lose? A slightly bruised ego? Let's take a look at how you can set up your goals by following the clarity through contrast model that I discovered on a blog site by a midwife named Christa Smith.

Your journal will come in handy for this exercise. Jotting down quick guides, ideas, and helpful hints in one place will help keep everything close for ease of access. You never know when you may need a reminder or quick reference guide. Fold the page in half and title one side with "clarity" and the other with "contrast."

1. List everything you want clarity on, which includes, and is not limited to career paths, relationships, building a new home, renovating your current place, financial strength, or focusing on your overall health, and wellbeing.

2. List everything that you are struggling with, that is causing you distress, or draining you of your energy and positivity on the "contrast" side which includes, and is not limited to examples such as long working hours with the rewards, or neglecting your health for the sake of others.

3. Read through the contrast side of your list and assess what you want to see changed or how you can turn a negative situation into a positive one.

4. Cross-reference your contrast list against the clarity side to see if you have a match that may look something like: "I am spending too much money on cigarettes" on the contrast side, and "I want to stop smoking."

Setting Clear Guidelines Based on Your Dreams

Eagle-eyed readers are going to accuse me of repeating information that has already been mentioned, explored, or discussed. Most of what is being repeated is important to each of the different chapter topics, and some need to be reiterated as gentle reminders. I believe that the more times something is spoken about, the more of an imprint it will leave in your mind. Whatever you are learning at the moment may not register with you until you see it mentioned or referred to in another context, and you end up with an *AHA* moment where everything falls into place.

This journey that we are on is about discovering your spiritual oasis, and the magical benefits you will be blessed with. There is no doubt in my mind that you have most likely explored many avenues that may not have been what you expected. This journey may not be what you wanted, but it did have something that resonated with you, and what you are experiencing during a specific season in your life. Maybe it is the fact that you are not being led around by a lead or that someone is forcing you to sign up for something you don't need. Maybe you are just in the right place, at the right time, and the universe has aligned to indicate that a new beginning is waiting for you. Remember that it is your choice and your life that you are redefining.

We are going to look at the guidelines which we have discussed previously. The difference now is that you are going to turn your previous page on its side, glance over with a fresh set of eyes, and a new perspective using the "clarity through contrast" technique. You don't have to feel overwhelmed or intimidated because you have all the basics down. We are going to re-enforce the walls with the knowledge we are gaining, to benefit you, and help you launch your dreams, desires, and intentions into the universe where they will land on the stars and start to manifest.

- Visualize that your dream will become a reality.

- Turn a wall in your house into a visual vision board so that you are reminded of your dream, and that you don't lose sight of what is important to you.

- There is a proverb that I believe was intended to be part of this guideline, which is also meant to eradicate self-doubt; if at first, you don't succeed, try—try again.

- Have more than one perspective; tap into all the chambers of your mind palace to visualize your dream becoming a reality, and you may want to give your gut intuition a pair of glasses to see your dream and send it off into the universe.

- Flood your journal with your dreams and desires, and keep putting all your energy into believing what you have written down.

- Continue with the positive affirmations and remember it is all about "I can do this," "I will do this," and "I will claim it as mine."

- Don't lose focus on your goals; continue adding, modifying, and doing whatever is needed to keep your dream alive.

Act as If

This point needed its own little bubble and explanation of what this means. People are quick to point fingers or tell you that you are jumping the gun or prematurely celebrating something that hasn't happened. A large part of manifesting your dreams and desires is believing that you will get what you want. It's okay to act as if you have achieved your dream. You are sending your intentions out into the universe, and letting it know that you will celebrate regardless of the outcome. Keep believing that your dreams will be recognized and that they will become a reality, and until that moment, act as if you have achieved greatness in your life.

I am going to share a list of techniques that you could implement into your dream menu when setting goals with the intention of implementing them. Don't hold back on your vision because you don't believe you have what it takes to be successful. You will never know what will happen if you don't take a giant leap of faith. You can't expect something to happen if you sit back with your arms crossed behind your head. Dare to dream, and dare to believe that something good will happen. I would also like to caution you that you are going to have to invest in a ton of patience when you apply the Laws of Attraction to your daily life. You have to constantly remind yourself that time moves differently in the spiritual world than what it does on earth. Having patience is a game that will benefit each player. It is a great feeling when your dreams and desires are realized because you will appreciate the results even more.

Use Your Universe to Reach for the Stars

You may agree that you are learning some valuable lessons during this ongoing journey to finding your spiritual oasis. I have no doubt in my mind that many find these lessons frustrating because of the constant tweaks and modifications along the way. I can tell you that no matter how badly you want a smooth journey, whether it is in reality or virtually, you will always encounter unexpected problems. It is important to remind yourself that you live in a fast-paced world where blinking may result in a major change or shift in dynamics. I know that it may be overwhelming and seem intimidating, and I know the anxiety involved in this process. Remember that everything you do—from setting goals to manifesting your desires—those desires—need to be kept current.

These practices are in place to ensure that you are secure on your universal pedestal. Standing on your universal pedestal will give you the courage you need to reach for the stars. You need to believe that you can reach the stars after applying the process of clarity and contrast. You get to hang your goals onto the stars, and believe that they will be recognized, and that you will be rewarded. Don't worry about reaching those stars if you can't get to them just yet. Your time may not be everyone else's time, and it gives you more time to learn some valuable lessons about finding your spiritual oasis. Let's skip over to the next chapter, where you are going to learn about manifesting your desires and implementing your very own menu based on your desires.

Chapter 6
Giving Your Desire a Voice

Have you ever witnessed a scenario where a child is trying to convince their parents that they "absolutely, most definitely, without a doubt" need a certain item or they could "literally die" if they don't get it? Most times adults will browse through Instagram and see an outfit, shoes, make-up, hair products, or gadgets, and announce to no one in particular that they need whatever is being showcased because it will make life so much easier. I would like to view these scenarios as desires, and verbalizing what we want and how desperate we are to get them, is us giving those desires a voice. Have I introduced you to my annoying voice of reason yet? I may have hinted at it during the Introduction, but yes, I have a voice of reason and that is that impulsivity leads us to spend unnecessarily.

I spoke with one of my researchers and they were sharing a story from when they were a child in the '80s. Growing up as an only child, they believed that money would grow on trees and that they could and would get anything they wanted—especially new toys that were introduced to the market. Their parents were involved in new product launches, and were always bringing new gadgets into their home—but none of the toys. One day, while playing at a friend's home, they saw an advertisement in a magazine for a new toy. The wheels were set in motion and the friends started campaigning for this toy. Remember, there were no computers so everything had to be done by hand, and very creatively too. They used a ream of paper, two sticks of glue, destroyed countless magazines and newspapers, and many tracks of staples to put their campaign presentation together. Their parents saw their hard work and determination during the process, which took a couple of weeks, and were prepared for the presentation.

At the end of the presentation, the two friends sat down beside each other, and waited for the outcome. Their parents left the room, and the friends agreed that they would be okay if the answer was no, and they would work hard to earn money to buy their much-desired toys themselves. When their parents returned, they each had a box in their hands, and they were given their toys. They were very happy, and excited, and shared their appreciation with each other, and their parents.

The moral of this story is that two eight-year-old children wouldn't have known about the Laws of Attraction, manifesting, energies, or desires. They would never have known that the term "Law of Attraction" was coined by an American author known by the name of Prentice Mulford between 1886–1892 (Wikipedia, 2018). What these two had done was something they worked on together. They had a vision, and they worked on their vision instead of begging, throwing tantrums, or giving their parents ultimatums. They poured all their energy into their desire to have this toy. They pitched their presentation to their parents, and both agreed that regardless of the outcome, they could still pursue their desires by working to earn money. This is the approach everyone, regardless of age, should strive for. They gave their desire a voice, and they were prepared for any outcome. If you are wondering—I did ask about the toys, and was told that they are still in possession of their toys. My interviewee informed me that their toy was en route to a family member as part of passing along their legacy of "patience is rewarded" philosophy.

The Voice of Reason: Manifesting Awareness and Attention for Your Desires

I have witnessed people expressing their desires about certain objects that they want. From an outsider's perspective, they aren't willing to do anything to get what they deeply desire. Part of me wants to jump onto the bandwagon and accuse them of being entitled, privileged and demanding something they don't want to work for. My voice of reason is very quick to wake up when I think about any bandwagons or being judgmental; it reminds me that people are easily misunderstood. I was recently at my local Costco and I spotted a lady in one of the appliance aisles. I could see her talking, and she was gesturing with her hands. The curiosity bug in me wanted to know who and what she was talking to. I casually started down the aisle, pretending to look for something, but also not wanting to miss any of her actions. I eventually made it within hearing distance, and I could hear things like, "one day, you will have a place in my kitchen," "I wish I could take you home right now," and "maybe you will go on special soon."

The lady turned to me with an apologetic smile and told me that she believes in verbalizing her intentions to people, animals, or objects. In this instance, she was talking to an air fryer. In most cases, people will rather talk about wanting a certain item, and express their desires instead of setting the wheels in motion. They could start this process by putting their desires out into the universe. I can totally understand that humans are impatient, and we want everything when we snap our fingers, but reality doesn't always work that way. That is why the bandwagon jumps into my mind and activates the voice of reason. I believe that although people are meaning well by sharing their wish lists and desires with others, they are missing an opportunity that would be challenging, rewarding, and educating. Would you like to learn how manifesting your desires could be all that and more for you? This is all part of the journey to finding and learning how you can share the treasures at your spiritual oasis.

Give Your Desires the Attention It Deserves

Think about the length of time it takes for you to perfect your looks before you leave your home. Think about the number of hours you put in at work to ensure your employer is satisfied. Think about every aspect of your life that you invest time, money, and energy into as you strive for perfection. How do you feel at the end of each of those tasks that you have achieved? I can only imagine how accomplished everyone feels as they glance at themselves in the mirror as they fly past, or proudly smile when their employers praise them for a job well done. Turn the wheel ever so slightly, and imagine how you would feel if you spent time giving your dreams, wishes, and heartfelt desires the same amount of attention and dedication.

You have learned how to set goals for yourself. You know that it takes hard work, dedication, and patience to achieve results. You know that you will be rewarded. Having and setting goals is something that needs attention. Think about the lady at Costco who was talking to the air fryer. The one-sided conversation she was having with it made me smile because she had the right attitude. We never discussed the goals she had set for herself, but the way she spoke about the air fryer leaves me with no doubt that she was doing everything she possibly could to get the air fryer she desired. I know, and I can completely understand that many people lose hope when their goals aren't being met, or their dreams and wishes are not being reached.

Let's take a look at a list of ideas that you could implement or add to your existing goals to spruce things up. You may never know, a reword here, a shuffle there, and a tweak everywhere might be what the universe requires to notice that you are still out there.

- Re-assess your vision board.

- Look at your goals through new lenses; change the way you think.

- Dream about your desires: Visualize where it will stand, how it will work, what you can do with it, or the smile it will bring to your face.

- Pretending is not only a game that children play; adults can pretend too, but don't allow it to influence your life.

- Tell a couple of friends about your desires; ensure that they are the right friends that will rejoice and be excited with you.

- Talk about your desires, and don't be afraid to talk to them.

- Write about your desires, and decorate the page with images of whatever your soul is yearning for.

Using the Law of Vibration to Fuel Your Desires

You have spruced up your list of goals, re-assessed your dreams, and made some changes to the way you think about what you want. We looked at a list that permitted you to revert to your childhood, it included a cautionary warning so that you don't lose focus of the ultimate goal, and allows you the freedom to change everything as your vision changes. You are now in a place where you are learning about manifesting your dreams. There is a whole lot more than just throwing your dreams and desires out into the universe and carrying on with your day.

I spoke to someone who is both religious and spiritual. I wanted to know how a religious person would feel about a spiritual world that focuses on what the universe brings to the table. I was prepared for a battle but I was stunned into silence by their response. I nearly changed the direction in which I wanted this book to go, but they asked me why it should be one or the other. I had to think about it for a moment, and then I realized that they were right. Everyone is always fighting about—this is right, that is wrong, you shouldn't do this, and you shouldn't do that. I assume that it is safe to say that we're all on the same page, and can agree that a higher power is involved. Who that higher power should or could be, depends on each person, and no one should be ridiculed for their choices. Things happen, people change, situations change, and everyone moves on with their lives and beliefs.

The Law of Vibration is something that is fueled by more than 7.8 billion people. Every single person that inhabits this earth creates more energy than any other source. These energies are put together by every emotion known and unknown to mankind. These are everything we feel which range from shame and guilt to pride and courage, including love, joy, and peace. Everything you emit into the universe is soaked up and fuels whichever emotion you are feeling. Your anger is feeding the anger in the universe, which cannot be anything good for you, or anyone else. Your joy and happiness is a seed that flourishes because of the love they can feel. This is what you want to strive for when manifesting your desires into the universe. What you want to do is fill the universe with good vibrations, and the perfect start is to give your desires the attention it needs. Let's look at some helpful tools that you can utilize to manifest your desires.

- Don't be afraid to ask for guidance on your journey; spend time in meditation, ask intentional questions, and listen to the voice in your head.

- Don't lose focus on what you desire; keep the flame alive by talking, imagining, writing, and thinking about it.

- Use your energy to put your desire out into the universe, and always stay positive.

- Throw your desires out into the universe where they will attach themselves to the stars until the time is right for your meteor shower to rain down its blessing onto you.

- Always be prepared for a failed outcome; try and try again until you are rewarded with your desire.

- Be patient at all times.

- Everything happens for a reason; you may not be happy with the outcome but the universe knows what needs to happen.

- Don't stop manifesting your dreams, goals, or desires; never give up on what is important to you or those around you.

Lean Into Your Desires

This has been an interesting chapter that reiterated a couple of points that have been touched on previously. It also offered much more insight into navigating your way to your spiritual oasis. The takeaway from this chapter is that it is okay to be fixated on something you want, but you should do your part in taking possession of your desire. I know what it is like to look at society and see how everyone gets what they want without working for it. We all have that special something that we want, and many of us know our limits (and balances), so we add them to the wish lists on online shopping platforms, or make mention of these desires in our journals, or even drop hints the family is in the vicinity. I keep thinking about the lady at Costco, and how she manifested her desires to the air fryer. I believe we can all take a page out of that lady's book. I do hope that she got her air fryer because that amount of dedication and faith should be rewarded.

Are you ready for the next chapter? The next step on our journey takes us from giving our desires the attention they need to opening the doors and allowing the manifestation to do the magic as it is intended. You are going to learn to have a little more faith in what you are capable of, and give yourself more leeway instead of putting a limit on the way you act, think, and do. The Pied Piper, that will be me, is ready to guide you over to the next chapter.

Chapter 7

No Place for Self-Doubt—Working Towards an Obstacle-Free Spiritual Oasis

We're our own worst enemy. You doubt yourself more than anybody else ever will. If you can get past that, you can be successful. –Michael Strahan

I believe that human beings are professionals in a sport that has not yet been recognized by the Olympic committee—mental gymnastics. We may all be over-achievers in this sport because we struggle with the choices we make. I have previously mentioned that everyone has a choice and they should do whatever they want. It is possible that even giving someone a choice could cause even more confusion. The quote tells us that we are our own worst enemies because we tend to take ourselves out of the equation. We are always thinking about what someone else will think about us, or how we navigate our lives.

Imagine standing at a crossroad where you are training for the upcoming Olympics. You want to go one way, but you are afraid that your first choice will be the wrong one. You want the gold medal, which is the direction that will lead you to the land of milk and honey. You have heard wonderful stories about this land, which makes your desire burn deeper. You are faced with an obstacle because no one ever told you that you had to choose a direction. What do you do? I strongly believe that all crossroads lead to the land of milk and honey. It depends on each person to make that land the dream you desire. Your mental gymnastics training is in full swing and you are ready to choose. However, you find yourself cloaked in a shroud of self-doubt just as you are ready to take that all-important step in the right direction. What do you do?

Using the Best Friend Code to Manifest the Abolishment of Self-Doubt

This chapter is about learning how to become your own best friend. I would like to introduce you to the "Best Friend Code" that I have found and modified to serve you. This code is meant to help bring out the best of you, which is exactly what best friends do. What would a "Best Friend Code" look like? I am so happy that you asked, and I would love to share some of the tips on my list with you:

- treat each other with respect
- treat each other with kindness
- always be there for each other
- always be honest with each other
- don't judge or berate each other
- banish all negativity from your mind palaces
- banish all hate from your mind palaces
- indulge yourselves at times
- look out for each other
- listen to each other
- always support each other

- always hold each other accountable

Some may glance at this list, raise eyebrows, and become one with the wrinkles from all the frowning. The list I have shared is something that we, as humans, adopt as part of our daily affirmations. We have to learn how to love, respect, and appreciate ourselves before we can expect others to show us any type of kindness. Every relationship should start with you because you are the main attraction. I am not saying that you should be walking around with a big head and an attitude that commands attention; I am saying that you should love, respect, and appreciate yourself before you can jiggle the vibrations of the universe to work in your favor. Let's go manifesting our desires with the Law of Allowing.

Resetting the Self-Doubt to Self-Respect

Self-doubt enters the conversation without any invitation from your mind palace. The fear associated with self-doubt trickles in through the weakened cracks. You may be arguing that you aren't afraid of anything, nothing phases you, or you just had a change of heart. Self-doubt is built around the fear of failure. Your family has dubbed you the barbeque king, and everyone has descended upon your home for a Sunday cookout. Everyone is singing your praises before you even warm up the grill, and the wheels in your mind start working. You start worrying about possibly burning the ribs or overcooking the steak. You look around at all the faces looking at you, and you are imagining the worst—that they are gossiping about you and that you are a failure.

You are allowing self-doubt to manifest itself in your mind. You are giving those thoughts, which are fears, the power to control your mind palace. Are you that person who worries about what others think, or who is imagining the worst-case scenario before an actual event takes place? If you are, I would like you to stop reading, and go back to Chapter 1 and read everything again. Everything that has previously been discussed has all been geared at setting you up for success. Every person that inhabits this earth owns a piece of the blue sky, the clouds, the rain, and the sun. Pull up a piece of ground, and claim your piece of the sky because you deserve to be here as much as the next person.

I want to take you through some of the steps that are going to help you navigate your way through your bouts of self-doubt. These steps do form part of the manifesting modules we have been learning about, which include setting goals and adopting a positive mindset. You will need to stop second-guessing yourself and your self-worth. You need to learn how to show yourself respect because you can't respect someone if you can't respect yourself. Think about the energy you release into the universe. Grab hold of as much positive energy as you can find, and fuel your desire to excel with the universal vibrations. I'm going to tell you something you may have heard before, and that is that you are allowed to be happy, excited, and feel worthy. You and your feelings, dreams, and desires are justified. You should never allow anyone to rain on your self-worth. It doesn't matter where you are on the spiritual journey to your oasis; you are allowed to have a slice of that sky I mentioned.

Reconnecting With Yourself

Manifesting intentions, desires, and dreams is a large part of your journey to your spiritual oasis. I've decided that I'm not going to give you one of my gentle reminders about what you should be doing to build up and strengthen your manifestation skills—not right now in any case. I want to show you that you are allowed to set your expectations high, and that you are allowed to believe that greatness is within your grasp. We need to break the mold that allows self-doubt, fear, and negativity to gain entry to our mind palaces. I want you to remember that you are in control of your thoughts and that your mind, body, and soul are important beacons in your journey through life. How do you feel when others force their ideas and opinions on you? The possibility is high that they are trying to influence you into thinking and believing that their way is the one and only—right?

Your spiritual journey does not mean that it is your duty to influence others. The only person you are going to influence is yourself, and the beauty of this journey is that it is on display for others to see. What is even better is that they will see a strong and determined person who knows what they want because they are not afraid to believe that they hold their beliefs in the palm of their hands. It is okay if people don't agree with what you are doing. It's okay to co-mingle with people who don't agree with you or see your vision. It is all about respect, and when you respect each other's beliefs, dreams, and desires—you are golden. Let's take a look at a couple of helpful tips that will help you understand the concept of being accepting of who you are and that you can manifest your desires without approval from others.

- The stars don't have to align for you to be happy and hopeful.

- Don't allow the hard times to snuff out your candle of hope.

- Don't be afraid to make the changes that are needed to ensure you achieve the desired results.

- Ditch the barrier of doubt that threatens to rob you of your happiness.

- Replace thoughts of doubt with "I can" and "I will."

- Be like the infamous Disney princess that tells everyone to "Let It Go"—minus the ice shards.

- Don't allow your obsessions to hold you back.

- Change your mindset where you focus on all the positives in your life, and shove the negatives out of your mind palace.

The best part about learning the art of manifesting is that you get to find what works for you. We have all heard the saying "practice makes perfect" but we also know that there is no such thing as perfect. I love this concept because you get to create your version of perfect that applies to you and your life. Go ahead, be confident, and create the life you want with your perfect imperfections. Now that's what I call manifesting the perfect reconnection module to your mind, body, and soul.

Removing the Obstacles in Your Way
I'm going to attempt to channel Michael Strahan by looking at his quote again. This chapter has taught you that you are your own worst enemy. It is one of those facts you want to deny, and you will try your best to prove that you are right and everyone else is wrong. The sad reality is that you are creating a barrier of denial around your heart and in your mind. Your mind is filled with doubt because you allow people to influence your choices. You become so afraid of taking that all-important step outside of your comfort zone, that you don't believe that anything good can happen to you.

I had a lengthy discussion with an interviewee who told me that they had always wanted to create a website. They wanted to use the website for blogging and sharing uplifting messages and some comedy with others. They also wanted to go into business with their sibling where they would jump on the trend of purchasing various objects and reselling for a profit. The siblings were excited to start their venture. The research started and they decided on a niche product that has taken the world by storm. Their plan was to start small on the product they wanted to sell and find a way to introduce the product without stepping on toes. The siblings had their long-term goals, which they set up, and each had short-term goals that would direct them to their ultimate goal.

A week into getting the website up for the blogging side of their venture, a friend approached my interviewee and told them that they should give up on the idea of writing because they were no good. This person was gutted because they knew they were good and, in the weeks leading up to putting themselves out into the world, they had wonderful feedback on a series they had developed on their social media platforms. The "friend" didn't seem to mind that they were crushing dreams that had been in the making for more than two years. They shared that their writing was good enough when they were writing professional letters and proofing work for the friend, but when it came to sharing the gift of words with others, their writing wasn't up to standard. Guess what? The website has been put on hold—yet again—because of fear.

It took a while to find the confidence to set the wheels in motion. The siblings were ready to move forward with the planning stages of their business venture. They discussed the website situation and concluded that they would proceed as originally planned. Walls of protection were being established that would keep the negative talk from derailing their plans. Unfortunately, another unhappy soul approached the siblings and told them that their idea to import and resell stock would be a logistical nightmare. They were also informed that they would not be able to fund their venture, and they would lose more than what they put into the venture. Fear entered the building, and the wall of protection tumbled down. They returned to the starting block, did more research, and changed their approach. The unhappy soul turned out to be an incredibly jealous competitor who had decided to play to the fears of the siblings. As my interviewee said: "To cut a very long story short, the unhappy soul lost everything because they were not willing to share the spotlight with anyone else."

The siblings have not given up on their dreams. They are actively working towards their goals. The website will make an appearance in the "blogosphere" in early 2023, and the business venture will be launched in November 2022. They will be pitching their products to close family and friends and grow from there. The takeaway from this story is that the siblings believed that it was their destiny to venture outside of their comfort zones. They had spoken about their dreams since they were little, and it took many years for them to stop resisting the universe. They set their goals, shared their intentions, and manifested their desires. Yes, they were affected by self-doubt based on what people they trusted were feeding them. I would like to go out on a limb, and say that the siblings have mastered the laws and arts of manifesting, allowance, and resistance. They have proved that one can conquer all fears. They may have been thrown off their game a couple of times, and yes, they may have thought about quitting, but they had goals that they had sent out into the universe. I believe that this is one of those testaments of faith where the universe was not going to allow them to give up on their dreams.

Michaels Strahan's quote ends with a statement that is worthy of being manifested into the universe. He is saying that if you can conquer the doubt barriers, you can be successful—I'm pretty sure he meant to say "when you can" and "you will be."

You be You, and Leave Everyone to Be Whoever They Are

It is such a wonderful feeling when you realize that it is not part of your job, family, or friend description to validate everyone, not be validated by others. You are exactly who you are meant to be—yourself. You are perfect as you are. Continue with your practice of manifesting desires, and be open to receiving your gifts. You are not responsible for those who don't understand the path you are following. I'm going to share a couple more manifestation tips to add to the lengthy list you have already acquired.

- Manifest your feelings and follow the prompts; the universe knows what you need, and will disperse your wants and needs when the time is right.

- Continue making lists, and include the people you love, the places you like to visit, the restaurants you love to eat at, and everything that makes you happy.

- Imagine the feelings involved when your goals have materialized; believe that you can see them, smell them, and touch them with your soul.

- Remember that "I can" and "I will" are important for your journey—claim your positive manifestation, and grab them with the energy you sent out into the universe.

- Allow your desires to manifest by believing, trusting, having faith, not resisting, and expecting the universe to reward you.

The final tip I would like to share straddles the line between Chapter 7 and Chapter 8. The best way for you to be successful and know that you are allowing your desires to be manifested—is to keep practicing positivity. Negativity is a time and energy thief that will rob you of what is important to you. Remember the sibling story that I shared, and how outside influences attempted to thwart their dreams and destroy their desires. They may have had a little stumble where they returned to their visionary board, tweaked their goals, and started again. They could have thrown in the towel and sent their dreams and desires to the rubbish dump, but they didn't. They chose to see the lesson that was presented to them, and they did what they could to turn those negatives into positives. Everyone—no matter who, what, or where you are—can have the same experience by allowing your desires to manifest in your life, accept, believe, and expel all negativity. Come on, let's go and scrub the negative thoughts and actions from your mind palace. As Babe Ruth, an American professional baseball player, said: "Don't let the fear of striking out keep you from playing the game."

Chapter 8

Side-Stepping Your Negative Thoughts

I'm not going to enter this chapter and proclaim that negativity will not be tolerated. I will be the first to advocate for positivity. Yes, we should surround ourselves with positive energies and people. Yes, we should send positive vibrations into the universe so that everyone can benefit. In a perfect world that would be exactly what the doctor ordered. As you may or may not know—we don't live in a perfect world. We do, however, live in a unique world where diversity is embraced by many, and disliked by many.

I know how hard it is to break the cycle of negativity. I have been part of that cycle, so have you, and so has everyone who lives and breathes among us. Negativity enters our lives when we are vulnerable. Family, friends, businesses, brand corporations, or influencers will feed off your vulnerability. Once they are in position, they will tactically begin to fill our minds with negative self-images, and the situation we find ourselves in. Is this scenario ringing any bells? Are any alarms going off? This is all too familiar, and yes, we have all been through this or something similar. This is a classic script that has been written and directed by bullies. If you have been here since the Introduction, you will know that I don't condone bullying, condemnation, ridicule, or any form of thievery that robs people of their dignity.

This chapter is going to be a rewrite of the original script. You get to rewrite the script based on your life, your journey, and your expectations going forward. Your script is not going to include family, friends, acquaintances, colleagues, or strangers. Your script is going to include everything you expect, dream of, and desire for and from your life. Come on, let's go and clean the chambers of your mind, body, and soul that have been caked in negativity.

The Implications of Being Encased in Negativity

Everything in life has its pros and cons, benefits and disadvantages, or positives and negatives. The gears in our minds are constantly working to find a happy medium that will suit everyone. A likely scenario would be that you want to resign from your current job because you don't like your colleagues, your boss, or the long hours that keep you from your family.

The positive side of your mind is saying:

- Your happiness is important.
- You could start looking for a new job to see what is out there.
- Speak to your boss and discuss the issues you are experiencing.
- You need to do what is necessary for you and your life.

The negative side of your mind is saying:

- No, you are not good enough to work in another position.
- You won't find another job.
- You will be miserable if you leave this job.
- Your family will be disappointed that you gave up your job.

- Forget about pursuing your dreams, they will amount to nothing—just like you.

The negative side of our minds doesn't want to see us succeed in life. It keeps trying to dictate the path we should follow. It becomes overwhelming, and we do lose focus, give in to our thoughts, and fall down a very dark hole that makes us miserable human beings. Have you ever been in that dark hole? Have you ever allowed your fears to override your happiness? I do believe that it is very safe to assume that you have been there, donned a couple of t-shirts, burned them, and clawed your way back.

The Side Effects of Negative Thinking

I met someone who told me about a family member who lived in a bubble where they believed that everyone, except for them, was negative. The person never had anything nice to say about anyone else, including members of their family. They had no problem turning their children against each other, and when confronted, feigned innocence and were quick to pack the blame onto someone else. One of the family members, who wasn't afraid to stand up to this person, told them in no uncertain terms that everyone has a choice. They told their family member that everyone holds their happiness in the palm of their hands. Each person has a choice on how they think about what they are given. Each person is responsible for their thoughts, actions, and reactions. People who choose to be mean to and about others because they want everyone to be miserable won't experience the joys of being happy. People who choose to be accepting, kind, comforting, or understanding will experience an abundance of happiness, joy, and elation that equates to the positive energy that is sent off into the universe.

You have to have a stern talking to with yourself to find out what you want. The choice is yours to make. Will there be consequences? Most likely. No one knows how the other person will react when you change sides. You should always remember that you can't please everyone. You have to do what is right for your mind, body, and soul. Even it means setting up boundaries and giving clear indications about your expectations. Trust me on this, your mind palace will be eternally grateful when you throw open the curtains, windows, and shutters to see the sun, and hear the chirping of the birds—sights and sounds of positivity.

The list I am going to share should not be used as a tool to self-diagnose yourself. I don't want anyone playing with their health, so I would highly recommend that you visit a medical professional for an accurate diagnosis. No one will judge you for putting your overall health and wellbeing at the front and center of your life. I stumbled across an article for the Cleveland Clinic. A psychologist, Scott Bea, answers questions about what he believes, on a professional level, the side effects of negative thinking could mean for your mental, physical, and emotional health (Cleveland Clinic, 2019). The list includes, and is not limited to the following disorders:

- anxiety
- obsessive-compulsive disorder (OCD)
- depression
- insecurity
- low self-esteem
- low self-worth
- worrying about everything
- panic

The Importance of Positive Thinking

We need to negate the negative side effects by focusing on the positives. The importance of positive thinking is beneficial to the quality of your life. I have previously mentioned a couple of hints and tips that will help you on your journey through life as you navigate your way to your spiritual oasis. You learned about journaling, affirmations, and meditation which promote positive thinking in your spiritual world. Everything that you have learned since embarking on this journey has been aimed at teaching you how to embrace a life free of strife and negativity.

I touched on the side effects of living in a bubble of negativity. Neither I, my editor, nor my publisher will judge you for being in this bubble. I want to gather all the knowledge and information I can find to give you a one-click guide that will not overwhelm and confuse you. I stumbled across another article that gave me an excellent overview of the benefits and importance of positive thinking. The article was written by Kendra Cherry and medically reviewed by David Susman, for the online publication, *VeryWell Mind*.

Stress Reliever

Stress is one of those little gremlins that mutate and causes undue worries. It feeds on anxiety, and will not hesitate to fill your mind with negative thoughts. You may think that it is difficult to control your thoughts, but it may be easier than you think. Changing how you think is going to take some work and skill from your side. Eliminate the stress in your life by forming new habits that will be beneficial for you—not for your family or friends—for you.

Improved Health and Wellbeing

You may have heard people speaking about how you should surround yourself with positive people, and that you should avoid negative people at all costs. This may be an unpopular belief, but something as simple as a smile or a helping hand, is a move in the positive direction. People that are consumed with negativity may take a while to understand their new feelings. They may be suffering from chronic headaches or suffering from a host of ailments that even medical professionals cannot identify. It may just be, and remember that I am not a medical professional, but it is possible that all their pent-up negative feelings are blocking their way to living a healthy, carefree life that is filled with joy and happiness.

Coping Skills

Everyone has developed a method that will help them navigate their way through the negative pools. I love finding ways to stop negative thoughts from invading my mind palace. I spent years, months, weeks, and days finding ways to cope with negativity that crept in through the cracks. You can control your negative thoughts. It is part of human nature to want to fly off the handle at the thought of something bad happening. We spend so much time looking for all the negatives in a situation, that we overlook the positive aspects. An example would be the war in Ukraine. The day the Russian army launched missiles, the rest of the world was sitting around their crystal balls and preparing for doomsday. I remember hearing the news, and my first thoughts were that I hope the men, women, children, and animals made it to safety. I sent out positive affirmations, prayers, and thoughts about everyone. I'm not going to take sides because I don't know the full story. I'm also not going to allow someone else to tell me how I should be feeling about such a volatile situation. Everyone develops their own, personalized coping skills, which help them see the scene from a different perspective.

Adopting a Positive Mindset to Assist Negative Thinking

Why would you want to help negative thinking? I'm so happy that you have asked, and I would be more than happy to tell you. Try as you may, negative thoughts will always enter your mind. We are surrounded by words such as no, not, can't, don't, won't, or never. If someone asked you for a quarter, your answer may be "no, not today" or "I don't have any change" which falls under the scope of negativity. Another likely scenario could be a spouse, a friend, or a family member saying, "I hope you have a good day," and your response may be something along the lines of "I doubt it because I have a meeting and everyone always ends up fighting." You fail to see the good in anything. The person asking for the quarter may want to buy a quart of milk for their child, but you didn't give them the opportunity to say anything. How do you know it is going to be a bad day if it hasn't happened? You don't know what is going to happen at the meeting? For all you know, someone may bring a dozen donuts for everyone to share.

We need to change your mindset. The previous section showed you how you could benefit from being positive. The examples that were shared are a drop in the ocean. I always encourage people to take the examples I give and modify them to create new ones. I've learned a lot of various people scattered across the globe who vary in age from toddlers to senior citizens. Look, listen, and don't be afraid to learn from others. You will never know what you will learn from someone if you don't have an open mind.

Breaking the Negative Thinking Molds
The first order of business is to break the molds that you believe define your life. You are going to transform yourself into Hulk and you are going to send the shards of negativity flying as you break free from your jail. You are not going to go back and pick up all the

pieces to rebuild the jail because from this point onwards, you are going to have an open-door policy when it comes to negativity. Part of the open-door policy is that you have to be honest at all times; whether you write in your journal or speak to a trusted friend, family member, or medical professional—get it out of your head. Identify the different types of patterns that have held you captive:

- anxiety, worry, and stress
- replaying past mistakes or errors in judgment
- believing that you will never amount to anything
- finding ways to keep the negative thoughts alive and active

Look at the four patterns of negativity that I have shared. I would like you to reflect on the items I have shared. Label them with whatever it is you are struggling to let go of. The next step of this exercise is to help you learn that you can turn your negative thoughts into positive thoughts that will be beneficial to your life and circumstances. As I previously mentioned, we can't stop negative thoughts, but they can be modified to serve a purpose.

1. Wave hello to the negative thoughts, but don't give them time to make themselves comfortable; usher them through the door as quick as possible.

2. You know how the negative thoughts make you feel; don't be afraid to expel them from your mind.

3. Don't settle for anything less than the best; enjoy the good, better, and best your world has to offer.

4. Negativity is one of those thieves who will take what it wants when it wants, and it doesn't care about the destruction it leaves behind; you get to take control from the thief and reclaim the focus that was stolen from you.

The Journey to Reclaim Your Misplaced Focus

We've reached the part of the chapter where we get ready to tiptoe over to the next chapter. We wind down after a loaded chapter where you are presented with a lot of information. This was a difficult chapter because I know that many people struggle with the thoughts that cloud our judgments. I feel very strongly about vulnerable people being taken advantage of. It makes me both angry and protective, which is another reason why I have undertaken to write this book in the manner that I have. I want my readers to be comfortable, and that they will know what to expect from me when I write more books.

I wanted to leave this chapter with more helpful hints to help you when you are trying to cope with negative thoughts. These are an added bonus that I discovered during my research, and which I knew needed their own space between the two chapters. I have put these hints into practice in my daily life, and it has helped me immensely; especially with anger, frustration, and patience.

- Set aside 10 minutes in your day to reflect on all the negative thoughts; after 10 minutes, you recycle them, and continue your day on a positive note.

- This is one of my favorite ones where when I have a negative thought or utter something negative, I immediately change it to something positive.

- Find the good in everything; just look around for things that make you smile.

- Form new habits, and phase out redundant habits that don't apply to your life.

- Establish a routine; people who have routines don't have time for negative thoughts.

Chapter 9

Reclaiming the Focus That Was Lost Along the Way

Focus on the possibilities for success, not on the potential for failure. –
Napoleon Hill

Somewhere between believing in the tooth fairy, the Easter Bunny, and Santa Clause, and adulthood, we grew up and changed. As a child, you are asked what your ideal job will be, and many will say doctors, marine biologists, veterinarians, professional sports people, or garbage truck drivers. Many parents may have encouraged their children by telling them that they needed to do well in school, and to reach for their dreams. Others may have told their children that they don't have what it takes to find themselves working in those fields. Have you ever seen a child who looks defeated when they are told that their dreams may not be realized? I have, and I can tell you that it is heartbreaking to see the light in their souls snuffed out.

Children mimic their heroes, but they do change their minds as they go through the stages of life. A child that wanted to be a garbage truck driver may decide that they want to join the police force. Another child that wanted to be a nurse may decide that they want to study arts and become a performer. Children grow up to become adults. The dynamics change because adults have a whole host of responsibilities that children don't know about. Some of us go on to college and earn degrees, and others don't want to study further and have dreams of doing something that will set them apart from others. The bottom line is that everyone has dreams, and those dreams don't always see the light of day because we allow negative thoughts to snuff out the light in our souls.

This chapter is about reminding you how to reignite the light in your soul. Everything you have learned throughout this book brings us to where we are now; subtle reminders and gentle nudges as we near the end of our journey to reach your spiritual oasis. Learning to manifest your desires and dreams has been a large part of this journey. You have learned how to implement many different techniques to help you realize your dreams. It would only be normal that you would want to add some modifications to everything you have already learned. The little details add to the strength and power you hold within yourself. Let's take a look at how you can bring the focus back into your life by rubbing the magic flame to reignite the light in your soul.

Giving Your Focus a Little More Attention

I believe that focus and thoughts have an "anything you can do, I can do better" kind of relationship. You set your focus on something you want, and your thoughts swoop in with their blinders and the connection is broken. You know and understand that you can't stop yourself from having negative thoughts. It's something that is in your DNA. You are very much aware of the fact that negative thoughts tend to cast a shadow over your happiness. We are going to perform a little maintenance on your focusing tools that help you manifest your dreams—or desires. I like to think of the negative thoughts as attention seekers who are looking for a way to escape a place where they don't want to be.

I mentioned the importance of having and setting goals in previous chapters. The goals, whether short-term or long-term, are there to help direct you to the ultimate prize. It is good to have goals, but it is even better when you envision those goals becoming a reality when you focus on them. I turned to the Merriam-Webster online dictionary for the definition of what focus is. The very first entry defines *focus* as being the central hub of activity, attention, attraction, a concentration point, or directing the focus onto something you are passionate about (Merriam-Webster, 2019). This is excellent advice from the dictionary, because this is exactly what manifesting is all about; you are focusing on your goals, and you are sending them out into the universe. Let's take a microfiber to your focus, and give it some well-deserved love and attention.

Focusing on Keeping Your Focus Where it Is Most Important

I read an article that was written by Dr. Richard Blackaby in which he says that our way of thinking is all over the place. He continues to say that we move from thought to thought without deciding on one specific topic. We don't give our thoughts time to get used to a specific topic because we are in a hurry to find something that we will find interesting. What we are doing is trying to cram so much into our minds that we don't realize that the thoughts expand and present us with more problems that we are not able to focus on. He mentions the term "multitasking" which is something many people consider an accomplishment, but is it really? Doctor Blackaby doesn't seem to believe it is. When you are sitting at your computer, and realize you need to pack the dishwasher, the phone rings and it's your boss, so you go to your computer to look for whatever they want. While on the phone, you decide that you need to boil the kettle for some coffee, but on your way to the kettle, you see that you forgot to sign the permission slip for your children's school outing. Doctor Blackaby points out that you may be trying to do everything at the same time which skews your focus. You end up feeling agitated and frustrated because you are not making the progress you had envisioned. It may be time to redirect your focus by completing one task at a time instead of starting multiple times to save time. You end up spending more time on your cluster of tasks and it sets you back in your time management (Blackaby, 2018). It may be time to retire the multitasking trophy you have awarded to yourself.

I like Dr. Blackaby's view of multitasking in the modern world. We know, and understand, that we live in a world that doesn't slow down. It took a global pandemic to force everyone to stop what they were doing. Many re-evaluated their lives and goals. Others walked around with a "couldn't care less" attitude. That is the closest I have come to seeing the gears grinding to an almost halt. The globe had a couple of months to heal itself while the scientists and researchers looking for ways to oil those gears and get everything on track again. Today, we are right back where we were more than two years ago, where everyone is trying to play catch up. Someone should probably break the news that no one will get back the time they lost. If you didn't do your best, work and focus on your goals, and send them out into the universe—you lucked out. The best news is that you don't have to wait for tomorrow because you can start over right now.

Manifesting the Shift in Your Focus

I wanted to share some uplifting ways which may help you re-evaluate your focus. It may be possible that you have some cobwebs that are blocking the flow of your focus. I do believe that it is a good idea to change your focus every so often. Most times we just need to press the pause button, step off the merry-go-round, assess the location we are in, and see everything from a new perspective. This is a painless process—I promise, and it won't disrupt the groove you currently find yourself in. you may be one of those that is asking a question I have seen and heard a lot which is "why fix something that isn't broken?" We aren't fixing anything; we are modifying our dusty mindsets that have lost their shine. We are going to refocus our focus by performing maintenance before we can make our way into the universe.

Decluttering

Decluttering exercises are beneficial for your journey through the spiritual realms to your spiritual oasis. You carry around a lot of debris that the world has tossed at you. All you know how to do is collect it, and pack it wherever you can find a spot. As much as your home, car, or office needs a good clean, so does your mind. Let's see what exercises you can adopt to clear those cobwebs and remove the debris the world has inflicted upon us to distort our focus:

- journaling
- spend time outdoors gardening, enjoying nature, or hiking
- spend time away from your digital devices
- meditate
- breathing exercises

Healthy Changes

This section is a continuation of the previous section, but with a couple of added ideas that needed their own paragraph. You have to do what is good for you, and not what others tell you. We have all been in situations where we are told to not lose focus or we will come last. Would it be appropriate to say that your happiness doesn't have to be turned into a marathon or a race? Everyone develops and processes life differently. Human beings come in all shapes and sizes, and no two people are going to be the same. We have previously established that what works for Ethel may not work for Lucy, and that is all part of the grand design.

Start your day by having a daily to-do list. Assign timeframes that work for you. Those time frames will be very helpful in managing your time efficiently. Did you know that daily to-do lists are the equivalent to your short-term goals, which help you focus on what you want to achieve?

Changing Your Attitude

Give your mind the gift of adopting a new attitude. Consider adopting the "I want" attitude, and getting rid of the "I don't want" one. Human beings are never happy with what they've got until they don't have it. We are quick to say what we don't want without considering that there may be consequences for our ungratefulness. We need to change our focus to always look for the positive side of the coin. Always remember to keep your intentions positive and focus on what it is you want to see.

New Day

Each day you open your eyes after a good night's rest is presented to you on a silver platter. You get to start today with a clean slate. Yesterday can't help you today, so you need to leave it where it is. Don't worry about tomorrow because you don't know what today will bring you. Focussing on today will help reduce your stress levels, you can do more when you aren't worrying about the past or the future, and you get to enjoy your day as if it is the last one.

The Show Must Go On

You can live in the bubble that you have created, or you can take a step outside and embrace your dreams. You have choices, some you knew about, and others you may have just learned about. You know that the show must go on, and that your focus needs to shift so that you can experience life without obstacles. Are you ready to bounce on over to the next chapter? We get to continue using the magic of focusing when we cross the borders. We also get to use our manifestation tools which include sending our dreams and desires into the universe. We then get to watch the firework displays as we wait for the magic to touch and guide our souls.

Chapter 10

Understanding the Essentials of Intention

One of the most important topics of this book has been about finding your spiritual oasis. The journey that followed has been one of cleansing, discovery, healing, and knowledge. The most important lesson that you learned was how to manifest your dreams and desires. The lesson that you learned was that you don't have to be afraid to have dreams and desires. If you don't add it to your wish list, you will never know what you will be rewarded with. You learned to finetune a couple of techniques that would present you with more options. I would say that one of the biggest takeaways from these lessons is that you were reassured that if at first, you don't succeed, try—try again. I want to present you with an addition to the manifestation corporation, and that is intention. I went to the Merriam-Webster online dictionary to see what they have to say is the official definition of intention. The very first entry in the dictionary defines *intention* as being about what you want and to what lengths you are willing to for your dreams to see the light of day (Merriam-Webster, n.d.).

The idea behind this journey to your spiritual oasis was to prove that you are the worthy recipient of whatever the universe has to offer. The universe is waiting for you to accept the gifts it has for you. Did you know that the universe is not asking you to sign up for a monthly subscription or donations? The sad reality is that human beings have been conditioned to believe that everything comes with a price tag. I recently witnessed one of my neighbors giving a boy a shoebox with art supplies and some soft toys. The boy looked at the box, and then at the neighbor, and back at the box. He looked at her again and told her that he didn't have any money to pay for the shoebox full of fun. That is when it struck me, right between the eyes, that even children are being raised with the belief that everything comes with a price tag. The neighbor reassured him that they didn't want anything in return. He took the box, gave the biggest smile I have ever seen, walked away holding his box of treasures, and said "thank you" until he was out of earshot.

The universe is not asking us for anything other than being good, doing good, and sharing the good with everyone we encounter. It is perfectly fine for you to lean into the universe and accept the gifts it offers. It's perfectly fine to ask for something you want. You may not always like the answers you receive, but that is just an indication that you didn't set your intentions as clearly as you could have. You get a pass to go back to the drawing board to modify your goals and set clear intentions. Don't allow life to put all your dreams, desires, and goals on the very last backburner in your mind palace where it collects dust and eventually become a memory. We did not go through the steps of spring cleaning your soul and mind palace for it to become encrusted with dust and grime because you are afraid of rejection. This is a gentle reminder that you have learned how to reset dormant goals, create new ones, and form new habits.

New Rules According to Intention Manifestation

I spent a fair amount of time stuck in quicksand—when I started working on this chapter. I found myself hemming–and hawing–and flitting back and forth to Chapter 9, where we spoke about focusing. Scattered between everything that has been discussed since the Introduction, Chapter 10 presented itself to me as a giant finger-wagging, doubt-planting obstacle. I finally stopped sinking when I realized that the topic of intentions closely mirrors the dreams and desires that have been discussed and mentioned multiple times throughout this book. I had to take a step back and step into the observation chamber where the eagle-eyed readers are standing around and watching every letter being typed. Many may be shouting at me to block those negative thoughts, and practice that I've been preaching. I agree, and I'm not going to make any excuses because I am not perfect.

You pour your heart into the goals you have and you release them out into the universe. You believe, with every fiber of your being, that your dreams and desires will come true. Goals, dreams, and desires may be part of your focus and what you want to achieve, but they may also be blurry visions of what you want because you are still unsure. The difference, when it comes to dreams and desires, is the level of energy you are sending out into the universe. Intentions are more powerful because your determination is stronger and more direct. Starting your day with intentions will help you receive the results you want because you are consciously going to think about the goal you set for the day. You will pour every ounce of positive energy into making the intention a reality.

Sorting Your Dreams and Desires from Your Intentions

You have been presented with a little masterclass about the meaning behind intentions. You may have experienced a moment of confusion because everything seems eerily familiar. All is well, and your journey to your spiritual oasis has not been derailed. You are still on track to arrive at your destination by the end of two chapters. We are, however, retracing some steps to fine-tune and modify some of the essential tools in your toolkit. I stumbled across a YouTube video that gave a short and sweet definition that I felt was well-suited for this part of the chapter. I do believe that this nugget of information will give you a confidence boost that will assist you on your journey to the ultimate goal. The definition, as presented by the narrator, is "intentions are goals mixed with passion."

The words "dreams" and "desires" have been used to help keep you focused and grounded on your journey. It has helped you to keep your eye on the goal. I have previously indicated that goals change so that you can keep up with your dreams and desires, and keep them current. You don't want to send them into the dust collector room of your mind palace. You are now going to sort through your dreams and desires, and then you are going to separate them according to the importance they represent to your life. Remember that this is about you and not those who are part of your life. This is where I am giving you permission, not that you need it, to be selfish and enjoy every tingling feeling you get when you are collecting your rewards on the other side of your intentions.

The New Faces of Manifesting Intentions

All your dreams, desires, and goals have been through the wash, rinse, and spin cycle. You may be wondering about the original lists and guides you worked on, and whether they were still relevant. The answer would be yes, nothing changes other than spending a little more energy on your intentions. You are working on your goals, and you have sent them out into the universe. The task you are learning about now is nothing you don't already know, but it does have some upgrades to help direct your focus toward investing more energy into your intentions. I like to start my day by spending at least half an hour on my daily affirmations and setting my intentions for the day. Everything is strategically planned so that I can offer the very best of myself to family, friends, colleagues, my pets, and myself.

It may seem like a lot of hard work to focus on setting daily intentions, but this practice is a lifesaver (and a relationship counselor). My experience has been positive because I realized that when I am constantly focusing on my intentions for the day, I am calmer, not as stressed, and people and my pets, enjoy being around me. I am not going to lie and tell you that implementing these new daily intentions happened overnight, or that it is perfect—it is not. It takes hard work and dedication. I had to adopt my own advice by keeping an open mind and trusting my gut instinct. I also removed negative phrases such as "I can't," "I don't know," and "maybe" from my vocabulary. I can tell you, without any hesitation, that I am enjoying this season of my life. I don't just talk about the topics I write about—I live it because I need to be truthful at all times.

Let's take a closer look at how intentions can be broken down and identified before writing them in stone. I do believe that it is an excellent idea to take a step outside of your comfort zone, and assess where you are on your journey. We tend to get comfortable in our grooves, and when that happens, we lose focus of the bigger picture. I know, and I can totally relate, to not liking changes, but sometimes a change is necessary to help us see that landscape instead of the portrait. My advice—don't allow fear to hold you back.

Identifying the Various Parts of Intention

It is part of human nature to want to analyze everything before we buy, use, or commit to it. The cautious side of your brain is always on high alert. Trust is an issue because everyone has had some or other negative experience that adds another warning signal to the alarm in our minds. You have been learning about manifesting your dreams and desires, and how to focus your attention on what you want. Now, I present you with a new addition which is known as intentions and closely mimics everything that has already been discussed. Trust me, I can understand why you are cautious and why you would want to know more. Let's identify the various parts of intention so that you know how to incorporate them all into setting your own intentions:

- beauty
- creativity
- love
- kindness
- open and accepting of all things
- no limit to what you bring to others or yourself
- the size of your intentions has no limits

Manifesting Intentions

You have been given a list of seven fragments of what intentions look like. The next step, after identifying the fragments you need to incorporate, is to have fun setting new intentions. The keyword here is to have fun. Setting intentions is not meant to be a brain-bending event. One of the recommendations that I have been seeing everywhere, and I have mentioned it in this book too, is that you need to put time and effort into focusing on your intentions. It is not a once-a-week practice; it is something that you need to do daily for it to be effective in your life. A very gentle reminder, with a nudge, is that your intentions are filled with positivity, which you are sending out into the universe. The more positivity you send up into the universe, the better your chances are of redirecting the positive energy to your spiritual oasis. Let's take a look at some helpful steps to help you set your intentions, and send them off into the universe.

- The first, and most important step is to only allow good and positive intentions into your life.
- Don't go looking for signs that your intentions are being heard; rather wait for the universe to give you the signs—trust me, when the universe talks, you will know.

- As much as the voice of reason annoys you; listen to it because it knows what it is doing.

- This may not be a popular opinion, but there is always a reason why things do go according to the way you want and expect; trust that all hope is not lost, and you will receive your gifts when the time is right.

Chapter 11

Energy Is the Power which Fuels the Universe that Feeds Your Spiritual Oasis

The energy of the mind is the essence of life. –Aristotle

This journey has been about discovering your purpose in life. Everything in this book has been worded, mapped out, and explained with you in mind. I wanted you to have a safe place where you wouldn't feel as if you were being forced to choose sides. I do believe that I have checked all those boxes without taking anything—other than an open mind and your time. I know that I had skeptics join this journey because they wanted to prove that you can't have a spiritual experience without adding religion into the equation. I wasn't going to make anyone choose something they were not comfortable with. My ultimate goal, which I sent out into the universe, was that everyone would have the freedom of choice to choose whatever made them happy. I didn't give you any options; I simply bombarded you with everything I could find to show you that you can find whatever you want in life, by throwing caution to the wind and believing in yourself. That's it—it's all about you.

Your spirituality is fueled by the energy you harbor in your soul. I am not referring to energy that is generated from the sun, power plants, or sugar. Your emotional and physical energy fuels the type of person you are, and it sets you apart from other people. Remember that I have repeatedly mentioned that no two people are alike, and that is because everyone possesses different energy levels. You may also remember that the energy you exude is received by the universe where it is recycled and returned to you. If you are going to be angry, you are sending anger out into the universe and it is sent back to you. You, in turn, feed off of that anger and you continue on your angry rampage. The good news is, if you have been following everything that has been talked about, you will know that you, and only you, have the power to change the dynamics. You are in charge of the energy that you send out into the universe.

The Power of Energy: Different Types of Energy

I found an article written by Becci Vallis for the online publication, *Rituals*. In the article, Becci interviews the co-founder of a health and wellness retreat by the name of Emilia Herting. The article is centered around a couple of different types of energies that affect our lives, and play a greater role than what we realize. Remember that your spiritual energies are used in conjunction with practices that have previously been mentioned which include, and are not limited, to yoga, breathing exercises, meditation, chanting, and journaling. I read a line in the article that stood out to me, and is the perfect summary of what energy is, and the importance it adds to our lives: "Energy is the source of life."

It is evident that everyone must fuel their energy supply. I am not oblivious to the fact that many people may not be able to do this due to illness, or limitations. It is up to each individual to bring their party packs to the party by spreading positive energy to those who may not understand what is going on. I recently had a lady tell me that their 94-year-old mother had dementia, and as the disease progressed, she became more difficult. She would swear, accuse people of doing things, and didn't have a nice thing to say about any of her children. The daughter told me that she had a choice; she could go into the care home filled with anger at her mother, or she goes in there full of smiles and dragging the sunshine in behind her. She knew that her mother wasn't able to think clearly, and by dragging the sunshine into the care home, being cheerful to everyone, and showering her mother with love, she was building up her energy supply. Let's take a look at some of the different types of energy, as shared by Emilia.

Mental Energy

Your mind palace is controlled by your mental energy. It all boils down to choices. You can choose to be positive in all areas of your life, or you can choose to be negative. Remember that you have two choices, and those two choices each, have two choices. No one can choose for you because it has to come from you. I can't tell you that you have to be happy all the time, and I can't tell you that you should feel miserable because you missed out on an opportunity of a lifetime. Continue practicing your techniques that have been mentioned previously, and try some others that may help you reserve some of your precious mental energy. Try the following exercise to strengthen the chambers of your mind palace:

- Find a quiet place

- Take a deep breath, in through your nose, and exhale through your nose

- Think of things to be grateful for and set your focus on them

- Take a deep breath, in through your nose, and exhale through your nose

- Go about your day by focusing on the things you are grateful for

- You are guaranteed to emit positive mental energy and infect everyone and every place you enter.

Soul and Spirit Energy

I believe that this is a very personal type of energy. Emilia describes it as having a close affiliation with the emotions that come from your spiritual oasis. The energy you are emitting radiates from deep within your heart and soul, and brings about compassion, love, generosity, and all things that showcase your spirituality. I would like to add a gentle reminder that the status of your spirituality does not define the energy you radiate. I know and understand that not everyone is spiritual, and many may not believe in anything supernatural or that there is something or someone greater than us out there in the universe. That is part of the beauty of this journey, as it is a one-size-fits-all kind of trek through the universe. No one is defined by their age, religious or spiritual status, gender, or ethnicity; here you are accepted for being a person who wants to do good in the world (Vallis, 2021).

Using the Power of Energy to Find Your Purpose

- What would you do if you were given an abundance of gifts that you would never be able to use in your lifetime?

- Do you stick it in a storage unit and forget about it?

- Do you go through everything and decide to share a fraction with others?

- Do you share it with everyone who crosses your path?

Imagine waking up each morning, and beside your bed is a basket of gifts. The note attached says that you should find ways to attract and share positive energy by using the gifts. Rumor has it that if you share your gifts, you will be rewarded with more than what you originally had. Let's take a look at ways in which you can multiply your supply of gifts by focusing on the positive energy that is forming a bubbling creek within your spiritual oasis.

Your Energy Levels

People are sensitive to others' attitudes or energies. If someone asks you for a cup of sugar, and you stomp around, slam the cabinets, spill half the sugar on the countertop, and thrust the cup at the person; they will know that it is not given with good intentions. They may just hand the cup back and say, "thanks, but no thanks." How will you feel?

I recently packed a bag with a packet of pasta, three bananas, three mandarin oranges, three apples, two onions, a sachet of gravy power, and a gallon of milk, and gave it to a friend. They didn't ask for it, they didn't expect it, and they called me when they got home to thank me. It was such a good feeling to give to someone without being prompted by anyone.

The moral of the story is that if you give with good intentions, you will be rewarded in other areas of your life. You may not receive those gifts today, tomorrow, or next month, but you will be rewarded when the universe is ready. Until such time, continue doing good so that the line of credit stays open and active. Should you be the grumpy guts who throws and slams things around? No, you should most probably look at realigning your relationship with your mental and spiritual energy. All hope is not lost, and you can come back. Everyone has a rough day.

Random Acts of Kindness

Doing good things for others, without any expectations, is a great way to boost your energy level. You don't have to be a philanthropist or a homeless person to do good for others. Most times, a smile is all that is needed to give someone hope that tomorrow will be a great day. Did you know that kindness doesn't have a price tag? It is one of those special gifts that you cannot buy at Target or Walmart. You cannot sell them on the Facebook marketplace or Amazon either. Kindness is something that can be found deep within your soul. First-time users have to dig very deep to find it, but it is there.

Identifying Your Purpose in Life

I have previously touched on this, and it is relevant when exploring the powers of energy in your life. The energy you emit is proving your purpose. Everyone goes through life questioning who they are, where they belong, or why they are in the positions that they are in. I believe that self-doubt is terrible negative energy that robs people of their happiness. You spend so much time thinking the worst of yourself and those around you, everyone is always finding fault with everything you say and do, or you just don't trust that anything good will ever come your way. In short, you are living in a bubble that is filled with toxic air, and negative energy and vibrations. That is a mindset that we want you to lose. You were born into this world for a reason, or a purpose. You may not know what it is, but you have a destiny to fulfill. You have a choice; either you can give up entirely, or you can pick yourself up and go digging around to find your purpose.

I want to give you a checklist to help you find your purpose in life. You may not find the answer you are looking for, but the answer will find you when you are ready to open your mind and soul. A little positive bomb from me to you; take a step outside of your comfort zone, look into your life, and look for the identifying pattern that shows you where your obstacles are—the ones that prevent you from seeing yourself.

- Don't be quick to give up on identifying your purpose; it is out there, so trust, and believe.

- Direct your focus to your goals, your zest for life, and your beliefs.

- Focus and intentions are two little tools that need to be practiced daily.

- Your purpose is not defined by a successful career, or by the size of your bank balance; success is measured by the type of person you are, or how you treat others.

- Your purpose in life is not measured by how much money you spend to help others less fortunate, or the donations you give; money will not help you when you leave this earth.

Identifying Your Purpose in Life: Gut Intuition

I needed to separate this one from the list I shared because it needs a little more attention. I have previously mentioned the voice of reason, which is another name for gut intuition, gut feeling, or "sixth sense." Every sense in your body will jump to attention when something doesn't feel right, when you have a good feeling, or when you get a telepathic message. I could be sitting at my desk, writing and doing research, when all of a sudden, I get the urge to call or text someone. I have learned not to ignore these gut intuitions, so I will send a message, and a couple of hours later, I may receive a response from the person saying that they needed the cheer. I know that not many people will agree with these feelings, but who am I to not trust my spirituality?

How do you know that your gut is trying to get your attention? I am so happy that you have asked, and I would love to leave you with a list to end this chapter. We will be moseying on over to the conclusion where I will give you some ideas and helpful hints to help you build and create a life based on the energy within your soul. But first, your list of tell-tale signs that will help you decipher whether your gut may be trying to communicate with you by:

- having a very clear vision about something that may be happening

- experiencing unexplained tension in your body
- having all the hairs on the back of your neck standing to attention
- experiencing goosebumps
- experiencing clammy palms
- sudden onset of nausea
- having recurring thoughts about a specific person
- experiencing a feeling that can be described as the blood draining from your body before someone with the bad news

Conclusion

We have reached the art of the journey where you get to sit back and reflect on all the information, hints, tips, guides, and stores that have been shared with you. One of my biggest goals was to give you a front-row seat where you were treated with the dignity and respect you deserve. I wanted to show and encourage you to follow your heart, and listen to your soul. This journey was never about me validating what others may have expected you to do, nor was it about forcing you to choose the direction in which your life goes. I showed you how to find your spiritual oasis, the bubbling brook, deep inside your soul that you have been avoiding. You know that fear has no hold over you because you are allowed to be, act, and think differently.

This was an open invitation for everyone to join this journey. The naysayers packed their notebooks to make notes about how I am forcing readers to sign up, donate, or join cults. Yea—no, I think I disappointed them there—sorry, not at all sorry! There were no ulterior motives or hidden agendas; just an outpouring of unconditional compassion for those who are being victimized for daring to think and act differently. Many read what I had to say holding onto their panic paddles, but they quickly learned that they had the freedom of choice. It is important to realize that we can't always please everyone. Your purpose in life is not to make people happy. The days where you were led to believe otherwise may have run their course after discovering that you are special the way you are.

Utilizing the Universal Outpouring of Energy to Create the Life You Deserve

I wanted to leave you with a guide that will give you everything that you will need to help you create a life that you are worthy of. The guide is not a summary of everything you have learned or seen, but rather a reaffirmation of identifying and tapping into the energy you hold within your soul. I do believe that it is important to remind you of the power you have inside of you. This is your "get out of fear" card, that allows you to live a normal life where you are the worthy recipient of the gifts the universe has to offer.

This will be the last time I am going to ask you to have an open mind and expand your vision beyond what you believe you deserve. Hold up your hands, and receive the gifts that the universe is pouring down on you. Those gifts are a testament to everything you have sent out into the universe. All you needed to understand was that positive energies will be rewarded with an abundance of gifts. Should you be sending out negative energies, and you don't like the returns; it is never too late to upgrade your moods, feelings, or energies. Remember that you hold your happiness in the palms of your two hands. You are the architect and interior decorator of your life. You get to decide what your structure looks like, and how you want to decorate it. You have no limitations, and you are in control at all times. Let's take a look at how you can create your best life by focusing on the energy you radiate, the type of person you are, and everything else you want to cram into your personalized guide to your perfect life.

Are You Living Your Best Life?

You don't need consent from me or anyone else to experience and live your best life. Everyone has different views of what their best life looks like which may include relaxing in front of the television, dressed in your oldest but most comfortable sweats, and armed with a large bowl of popcorn, Reese's pieces, and caramel M&Ms mixed together. Who is anyone to judge you for wanting to relax and indulge in your favorite treats? Others may regard hiking to the top of Mount Timpanogos in Utah as part of living their best life. Your best life is based on what YOUR passion is, and not what your partner, family, or friends tells you it should be.

How can you tell if you are living your best life? Are you perhaps stuck in a rut? Let's take a look at some helpful pointers to help you determine whether you are just living your life, or whether you are living your best life.

- Be who you are meant to be; don't reserve the best of yourself for a select group of people—share yourself with everyone.

- Pay close attention to your actions, and thoughts; you have more control than you realize.

- Don't let your bad habits cause obstacles that prevent you from striving for your best.

- Visualize the life you want to live and be the person you are meant to be.

The Stepping Stones to Your Pedestal

This is where all the breadcrumbs are collected and put together for your pedestal. This pedestal is very special in terms of its location. It is located at the bubbling brook of your spiritual oasis. Your pedestal was designed for you, by yourself, and is indestructible for as long as you continue feeding your oasis with positive energy, or at least making an effort to do the best that your abilities will permit. Remember that this is not a quick fix remedy or a Band-Aid for whatever is going on in your life. This is a way of life that you need to work at to reach your desired result of creating your best life.

- Don't lose focus on your dreams and desires.

- Passing the buck is a game people play when they don't want to take responsibility for their actions; don't be that person.

- A subtle, yet firm reminder that you can't do anything to change yesterday, and tomorrow hasn't happened yet; live for today because it is here right now.

- Be mindful of your attitude towards others because you don't know what the next person is going through to be in the position they are in.

- Don't be afraid to declutter areas of your life that need a thorough cleaning.

- Show appreciation for everything you are gifted.

- Step up on your journaling journey.

- Do service in your community and be rewarded with a smile that reaches the eyes.

- Stop beating yourself up for making mistakes; there is a reason for everything that happens.

- Goals, intentions, and habits do change, and you need to have an alternative route for plans that change.

- Don't be afraid to go back to the drawing board, erasing all your goals, dreams, desires, and intentions, and starting over; change is good for the mind, body, and soul.

Taking Care of Your Mind, Body, and Soul

I am not here to body shame anyone, nor am I going to tell you how to manage your lifestyle. Some people need a reminder that the bowl of popcorn full of candy is meant to be a treat and not part of their daily diet. No one is going to tell you that you should never indulge in treats, alcohol, or anything that may negatively affect your health and wellbeing. Create a healthy balance by eating food that will nourish your body, and limit treats for special occasions.

Incorporate exercise into your daily life. You don't need to go to the gym, but you have a wealth of options that you can do from the comfort of your home, which includes:

- dancing
- Pilates
- yoga
- gardening
- sweeping your home
- vacuum cleaning
- having an under-the-desk treadmill while working

Introducing the Gifts From the Comfort of Your Best Life Pedestal

The best, and most valuable gift, you can give to yourself and those around you—is to be humble at all times. Don't be who you are not because eagle-eyed individuals will see through the cracks you are trying to cover. You may encounter people who don't agree with what you are doing, or how you are living your life, but that should not present a problem to you. I have previously mentioned (many times), that you are not here to please everyone. No one, especially the ones who are running you down, knows what your purpose in this life is. You have a lot of growing to do until your purpose is revealed. Everything I have mentioned throughout this book, and the refresher guide in the Conclusion, are the directions to prepare you for your purpose.

You get to have fun, and live your best life with help and guidance from the universe. You are acquiring invaluable life lessons along the way. You get to create a life that fits in with your time frame. You are no longer restricted by "you can't," "you shouldn't," or "don't." Here is the best news you have heard before, but it needs to be said again; you get to live your best life without any guilt. Let's take a look at some of the gifts that form part of the bubbling brook at your spiritual oasis.

The Gift of Forgiveness
You have the opportunity to forgive those who have hurt you. You are not expected to forget what has happened, but forgiving someone is healing for your mind, body, and soul. You release the anger that is blocking your direct line to the universe.

The Gift of Gratitude
We live in a world where people take kindness for granted. When someone is presented with something, they are quick to dismiss that gift, or even expect more. We need to spend more time being grateful for what we have got, than angry or lustful for what we don't have. I would like to express my gratitude by thanking you for your time, and for joining me on this journey.

The Gift of Patience
We are always in a hurry to get things done yesterday. We do forget that yesterday can't do much for today, but when it comes to our patience levels, all is forgotten. Patience has a way of bringing out the worst in people who can't get what they want when they snap their fingers. Those who forget how patience works don't realize that "a watched pot never boils" and "good things come to those

who wait." A quick trip down Proverb Lane will give you the advice you need to deal with patience.

The Bubbling Brook of Your Spiritual Oasis

You have the freedom of choice to create your best life based on whatever fits in with what you believe and strive for. You don't need me, or anyone else to tell you how to live your best life. Nobody knows you better than you know yourself. The beauty of being in charge of creating your best life is that you can add, remove, and rearrange your best life to suit you. You won't know how you will feel tomorrow, or you may not know what your life will present you with three months down the line. Always remember that we live in an ever-changing, fast-paced world that doesn't slow down because we're having a slumpy kind of day.

All Roads End at the Bubbling Brook

You have finally arrived at your destination. Thank you for joining me on this journey to uncover your spiritual oasis. I am feeling confident that I have presented you with more information than you realized there would be. You don't have to strive for perfection in this world, but you are perfect in your world. You are unique, and no one can take that away from you.

I hope you have enjoyed spending time with me. I will leave my PayPal and Venmo details for you to sign up for a monthly subscription, or even for donations. Dear Naysayers—I'm joking! It may be time to retire your pens and notepads after this book. May I be so forward as to ask you to please review this book on Amazon or any of the platforms where you may find it? And please do feel free to reach out and share your spiritual journey with me and other readers.

Until we meet again… Please be safe, and love the life you have.

Thanks For Reading

I'd greatly appreciate it if you took just a moment to leave an honest review on Amazon. If you don't have the time to leave a review, a simple rating will work just fine. Every bit helps.

Thank you for your support!

Also, don't forget your **FREE** gift! Just scan the code below.

References

A quote by Babe Ruth. (n.d.). Goodreads. https://www.goodreads.com/quotes/749690-don-t-let-the-fear-of-striking-out-keep-you-from

A quote by Ray Bradbury. (n.d.). Goodreads. https://www.goodreads.com/quotes/547018-love-what-you-do-and-do-what-you-love-don-t

Abundance No Limits. (n.d.). *What are the 7 laws of attraction?* Abundance No Limits. https://www.abundancenolimits.com/what-are-the-7-laws-of-attraction/

Aguirre, P. (2017, June 10). *The three pillars of human spirituality.* AToN Center. https://www.atoncenter.com/the-three-pillars-of-human-spirituality/

Alana. (2018, August 16). *How hiding your most valuable inner treasures holds you back.* Medium. https://medium.com/healthy-mind-healthy-life/how-hiding-your-most-valuable-inner-treasures-holds-you-back-5a0c1ad46c67

The Aligned Life. (2018, April 28). *What is an intention? | manifestation techniques | the aligned life | mindset + manifesting* [Video]. YouTube. https://www.youtube.com/watch?v=cLqTZ8Cvnvg&t=71s

Antill, J. (2018, February 23). *Why it's important to give your desires the attention they deserve.* Wonder Forest. https://www.thewonderforest.com/important-give-desires-attention-deserve/

Aristotle quotes. (n.d.). BrainyQuote. https://www.brainyquote.com/quotes/aristotle_377764

Baksa, P. (2011, October 5). *Attract anything you want through focused intention?* HuffPost. https://www.huffpost.com/entry/laws-of-attraction_b_910461

Barnes, L. (2018, January 15). *Spiritual healing: Steps to heal yourself naturally.* Raising Self Awareness. https://raisingselfawareness.com/spiritual-healing-steps/

Blackaby, R. (2018, September 24). *The incredible power of focus.* Dr. Richard Blackaby. https://www.richardblackaby.com/the-incredible-power-of-focus/

Brian Tracy International. (2018, December 12). *The power of your subconscious mind.* Brian Tracy. https://www.briantracy.com/blog/personal-success/understanding-your-subconscious-mind/

Budd, K. (2020, September 4). *Inner treasures: Positive perspectives & practices to incorporate into your life.* Chopra. https://chopra.com/articles/inner-treasures-positive-perspectives-practices-to-incorporate-into-your-life

Calef, S. (n.d.). *Dualism and mind.* Internet Encyclopedia of Philosophy. https://iep.utm.edu/dualism-and-mind/

Canfield, J. (2021, September 8). *A complete guide to using the law of attraction.* Jack Canfield. https://jackcanfield.com/blog/using-the-law-of-attraction/

Caprino, K. (2018, November 28). *Three simple steps to identify your life purpose and leverage it in your career.* Forbes. https://www.forbes.com/sites/kathycaprino/2018/11/28/t

hree-simple-steps-to-identify-your-life-purpose-and-leverage-it-in-your-career/?sh=440fece8695f

Cherry, K. (2020, June 1). *Benefits of positive thinking for body and mind.* Verywell Mind; Verywellmind. https://www.verywellmind.com/benefits-of-positive-thinking-2794767

Christian, L. (2020, October 26). *Taking action: 15 Smart ways to go from dreaming to doing.* SoulSalt. https://soulsalt.com/taking-action/

Cioban, A. (2017, January 21). *Seven steps to allow your desire to manifest.* LA Yoga Magazine - Ayurveda & Health. https://layoga.com/practice/spirituality/seven-steps-to-allow-your-desire-to-manifest/

Clemente, S. P. (2021, November 7). *Rising through resilience: Suteja of inner treasure hunt on the five things you can do to become....* Authority Magazine. https://medium.com/authority-magazine/rising-through-resilience-suteja-of-inner-treasure-hunt-on-the-five-things-you-can-do-to-become-9dba7f28779

Cleveland Clinic. (2019, October 3). *How to turn around your negative thinking.* Cleveland Clinic; Health Essentials from Cleveland Clinic. https://health.clevelandclinic.org/turn-around-negative-thinking/

Cohen, J. (n.d.). *How to quickly discover your inner treasure.* SolveYourProblem. https://solveyourproblem.com/page/view-post?id=464

Conley, B. (2022, January 8). *Four keys to your healing.* Bayless Conley. https://baylessconley.tv/four-keys-to-your-healing/

Cooper, K. (2015, March 2). *Law of attraction and allowing: 3 Tips for getting out of your own way.* Live Life Made to Order. https://www.livelifemadetoorder.com/blog/law-of-attraction-and-allowing/

Corbin, K. (n.d.). *The magic of focus.* SelfGrowth.com. https://www.selfgrowth.com/articles/the-magic-of-focus

Cuncic, A. (2020, June 29). *How to change your negative thought patterns when you have SAD.* Verywell Mind. https://www.verywellmind.com/how-to-change-negative-thinking-3024843

Davis, T. (n.d.). *Taking action: 8 Key steps for acting on your dreams.* The Berkeley Well-Being Institute. https://www.berkeleywellbeing.com/taking-action.html

Duroy, D. (2021, July 2). *Changing your life through the art of allowing — Living in manifestation.* Medium. https://dduroy.medium.com/changing-your-life-through-the-art-of-allowing-living-in-manifestation-f5a5256aba6c

Dyer, W. W. (2015, October 16). *Manifesting 101: The art of creating a life you love.* Dr. Wayne W. Dyer. https://www.drwaynedyer.com/blog/manifesting-101-mastering-the-art-of-getting-what-you-want/

Eatough, E. (2021, November 5). *Out-of-sorts? Strengthening your mind, body, soul connection can help.* Betterup. https://www.betterup.com/blog/mind-body-and-soul

Edberg, H. (2021, February 24). *How to take action: 12 Habits that turn dreams into reality.* The Positivity Blog. https://www.positivityblog.com/how-to-take-action/

The Editors. (2020, June 30). *10 Tips for living your best life*. Chopra. https://chopra.com/articles/10-tips-for-living-your-best-life

Fearless Soul. (2017, March 23). *The power of intentions - this video might change everything!* [Video]. YouTube. https://www.youtube.com/watch?v=ewB2Xv9WFpw&t=35s

Forbes Coaches Council. (2016, May 9). *Council post: 13 Ways to overcome negative thought patterns*. Forbes. https://www.forbes.com/sites/forbescoachescouncil/2016/05/09/13-coaches-explain-how-to-overcome-negative-thought-patterns/?sh=25fa3ce735cb

Forleo, M. (2012, September 18). *How to reprogram your subconscious mind to get what you want*. Marie Forleo. https://www.marieforleo.com/blog/how-to-reprogram-your-subconscious-mind

Fox, M. (n.d.). *These 12 universal laws will help you to manifest everything*. SelfMadeLadies by Mia Fox. https://selfmadeladies.com/universal-laws/

Frick, M. (2020, December 30). *Setting intentions to manifest the life you want*. Daily Mom. https://dailymom.com/shine/setting-intentions-to-manifest-the-life-you-want/

Gabriel, R. (2018, November 2). *8 Ways of manifesting your desires*. Chopra. https://chopra.com/articles/8-steps-to-manifesting-your-desires

Garnett, T. (2012, September 18). *The power of focus: Directing your life with intention*. Tiny Buddha. https://tinybuddha.com/blog/the-power-of-focus-directing-your-life-with-intention/

Gower, L. (2022, July 3). *How to live your best life starting today.* Lifehack. https://www.lifehack.org/863545/live-your-best-life

Grainger, C. (2022, May 15). *What is the law of attraction?* Brides. https://www.brides.com/what-is-the-law-of-attraction-5187044

Gulino, E. (2020, August 28). *I asked a witch about manifesting & it made me realise I've been doing it all along.* Refinery29. https://www.refinery29.com/en-gb/how-to-manifest

Hughes, G. (2019, November 7). *How to reprogram your subconscious and change your life.* Medium. https://medium.com/@geoffhughes94/how-to-reprogram-your-subconscious-and-change-your-life-c9af5a142d88

Ilse. (2022, February 21). *How you can start living your best life! - 10 Tips & tools.* Digital Travel Couple. https://digitaltravelcouple.com/how-you-can-start-living-your-best-life/

Jack Canfield quote. (n.d.). A-Z Quotes. https://www.azquotes.com/quote/714665

Jennifer. (2018, August 30). *How to get in receiving mode for what you want.* Jennifer365. https://jennifer365.com/blog/how-to-get-in-receiving-mode

Keithley, Z. (2021, July 28). *What is the art of allowing? (A complete guide).* Zanna Keithley. https://zannakeithley.com/what-is-the-art-of-allowing/

Kelly, V. (2014, September 16). *The girl code: 23 Things every BFF should know.* Sofeminine.

https://www.sofeminine.co.uk/personal-life/the-girl-code-23-things-every-bff-should-know-s1014471.html

Leigh. (2016, July 13). *How to find your core desires and the passion to pursue them | lifeos.* Life Operating System. https://lifeoperatingsystem.com/how-to-find-your-core-desires-and-the-passion-to-pursue-them/

Lipton, B. (2015, April 25). *Is there a way to change subconscious patterns?* Bruce Lipton. https://www.brucelipton.com/there-way-change-subconscious-patterns/

Losier, M. J. (2019, August 9). *When you give attention, energy and focus to your desire, it causes you to send the vibration of what you gave attention to. Yes, it is that easy.* LinkedIn. https://www.linkedin.com/pulse/when-you-give-attention-energy-focus-your-desire-causes-losier/

Lynch, M. (2022, February 22). *How to get yourself to take action towards your goal.* Lifehack. https://www.lifehack.org/878426/take-action

Makani, H. (2020, July 19). *The power of self love.* Times of India Blog. https://timesofindia.indiatimes.com/readersblog/i-think-a-lot/the-power-of-self-love-23336/

Mayo Clinic Health System staff. (2020, July 8). *7 Tips to live a happier life.* Mayo Clinic Health System. https://www.mayoclinichealthsystem.org/hometown-health/speaking-of-health/7-tips-to-live-a-happier-life

McGinley, K. (2015, December 31). *Intention, attention, no tension: 3 Tips to master the law of attraction.* Chopra. https://chopra.com/articles/intention-attention-no-tension-3-tips-to-master-the-law-of-attraction

Merriam-Webster. (n.d.). Intention. In *Merriam-Webster.com dictionary*. Retrieved July 28, 2022, from https://www.merriam-webster.com/dictionary/intention

Merriam-Webster. (2019). Focus. In *Merriam-Webster.com dictionary*. Retrieves July 22, 2022, from https://www.merriam-webster.com/dictionary/focus

Mia. (2019, October 6). *How to take action on your dreams*. She Dreams All Day. https://shedreamsallday.com/how-to-take-action-on-your-dreams/

Michael Strahan quotes. (n.d.). BrainyQuote. https://www.brainyquote.com/quotes/michael_strahan_644475

MindTools. (2009). *AIDA: Attention-Interest-Desire-Action Inspiring action with your writing*. Mindtools. https://www.mindtools.com/pages/article/AIDA.htm

Napoleon Hill quote. (n.d.). A-Z Quotes. https://www.azquotes.com/quote/781462

Nea. (n.d.). *Law of attraction - allowing v.s. resisting manifestation - universal laws*. Attraction Saga. https://www.attractionsaga.com/lawofattraction-allowing.html

O'Brien, M. (2018, August 20). *4 Keys to overcoming negative thinking for good*. Mrs. Mindfulness. https://mrsmindfulness.com/the-four-keys-to-overcoming-negative-thinkingfor-good/

Olsson, R. (2021, June 26). *Take care of your body, mind and spiritual health*. Banner Health. https://www.bannerhealth.com/healthcareblog/better-me/8-ways-to-take-care-of-your-spiritual-health

Page, S. (2021, November 8). *How the benefits of positive thinking will help your mind & body.* TotalWellness. https://info.totalwellnesshealth.com/blog/benefits-of-positive-thinking

Pangilinan, J. (2022, January 20). *91 Spiritual quotes to awaken and enrich your life.* Happier Human. https://www.happierhuman.com/spiritual-quotes/

Patel, D. (2019, May 8). *9 Ways to attract good energy today and every day.* Entrepreneur. https://www.entrepreneur.com/article/332544

Patnaik, T. (2022, April 25). *Benefits of spirituality.* Medindia. https://www.medindia.net/patients/lifestyleandwellness/benefits-of-spirituality.htm

Pavlina, S. (2005, October 17). *Cause-Effect vs. intention-manifestation.* Steve Pavlina. https://stevepavlina.com/blog/2005/10/cause-effect-vs-intention-manifestation/

Poddar, S. (2018, June 28). *Take action… Implement your dreams!* Ascent Publication. https://medium.com/the-ascent/take-action-implement-your-dreams-2f629cf378b3

Rampton, J. (2018, February 13). *10 Ways to turn your life around for the better.* Entrepreneur. https://www.entrepreneur.com/article/308759

Raypole, C. (2021, January 27). *Trust your gut: What it actually means.* Healthline. https://www.healthline.com/health/mental-health/trust-your-gut

Regan, S. (2022, April 27). *Manifestation gets a bad rap: Allow us to explain what it really entails.* MindBodyGreen. https://www.mindbodygreen.com/articles/manifestation

Richards, C. (2016, June 2). *Reprogramming your subconscious mind.* UPLIFT. https://uplift.love/reprogramming-your-subconscious-mind/

Richards, K. (2021, July 28). *The power of intention in manifestation.* Medium. https://kelli-richards.medium.com/the-power-of-intention-in-manifestation-1172aeb8daf6

Robyn. (2018, October 15). *Finding your bhavana: How to create desire when you don't know what you want.* Nomads with a Purpose. https://www.nomadswithapurpose.com/finding-your-bhavana-how-to-create-desire-when-you-dont-know-what-you-want/

Roland, O. (2021, July 13). *Book review: The power of intention — how to co-create your world.* Medium. https://olivierrolanden.medium.com/book-review-the-power-of-intention-how-to-co-create-your-world-9f8d3d4942a0

Sang, A. (2022, April 29). *9 Practical tips for living your best life now.* Clever Girl Finance. https://www.clevergirlfinance.com/blog/living-your-best-life/

Santi, J. (2022, February 21). *The everygirl's guide to manifestation and achieving your best life.* The Everygirl. https://theeverygirl.com/manifestation-guide/

Sawhney, R. (2018, February 27). *The magical power of focus.* LinkedIn. https://www.linkedin.com/pulse/magical-power-focus-rinku-sawhney/

Scott, E. (2020, August 3). *5 Self-care practices for every area of your life.* Verywell Mind; Verywell Mind. https://www.verywellmind.com/self-care-strategies-overall-stress-reduction-3144729

Scott, S. (2019, July 8). *How to be happy.* Happier Human. https://www.happierhuman.com/difference-religion-spirituality/

Simonova, L. (2020, March 14). *10 Types of spirituality and spiritual practices.* Happier Human. https://www.happierhuman.com/types-spirituality/

Smith, C. (2017, October 1). *How to use the clarity through contrast technique.* Christa Smith. https://www.christa-smith.com/use-clarity-through-contrast-technique/

Smith, E. (2016, September 7). *Spiritual wellness: What is your meaning and purpose?* LHSFNA. https://www.lhsfna.org/spiritual-wellness-what-is-your-meaning-and-purpose/

Sparks, R. (2018, May 9). *7 Steps to discover your purpose.* Thrive Global. https://thriveglobal.com/stories/7-steps-to-discover-your-purpose/

Spiritual counseling training: Intention manifestation. (n.d.). UniversalClass. https://www.universalclass.com/articles/spirituality/spiritual-counseling-training-intention-manifestation.htm

Sterr_ee. (n.d.). *Law of attraction: How I manifest my desires.* We Heart It. https://weheartit.com/articles/347685686-law-of-attraction-how-i-manifest-my-desires

Team Tony. (2017, February 9). *6 Strategic tips to reprogram your mind.* Tony Robbins. https://www.tonyrobbins.com/mind-meaning/how-to-reprogram-your-mind/

Tewari, A. (2021, June 9). *9 Steps to manifest what you really want in life.* Gratitude - the Life Blog. https://blog.gratefulness.me/how-to-manifest-2/

12 Universal laws for manifestation. (2019, September 6). Ladies Up. https://www.ladiesup.co/blog-1/2019/9/6/12-universal-laws-for-manifestation

Vadlamani, S. (n.d.). *8 Manifestation techniques: Understanding the law of attraction.* Happiness.com. https://www.happiness.com/magazine/personal-growth/manifestation-techniques-the-law-of-attraction

Vallis, B. (2021, March 8). *All the different types of energy.* Rituals. https://www.rituals.com/en-nl/mag-rituality-types-of-energy.html

Vantage Fit. (2021, November 11). *5 Ways to reprogram your subconscious mind and unleash it's power.* Vantage Fit-Corporate Wellness Blog. https://blog.vantagefit.io/reprogram-your-subconscious-mind/

Waters, S. (2022, April 12). *Benefits of positive thinking: 10 Ways to improve life with optimism.* Betterup. https://www.betterup.com/blog/positive-thinking-benefits

Wiest, B. (2018, September 12). *13 Ways to start training your subconscious mind to get what you want.* Forbes. https://www.forbes.com/sites/briannawiest/2018/09/12/13-ways-to-start-training-your-subconscious-mind-to-get-what-you-want/?sh=6776edbb7d69

Wikipedia. (2018, November 15). *Prentice Mulford.* Wikipedia; Wikimedia Foundation. https://en.wikipedia.org/wiki/Prentice_Mulford

Wilding, M. (2022, March 10). *How to stop overthinking and start trusting your gut*. Harvard Business Review. https://hbr.org/2022/03/how-to-stop-overthinking-and-start-trusting-your-gut

Yadav, K. (2020, July 12). *Duality of mind*. Medium. https://medium.com/@karishmayadav276/duality-of-mind-219bc4003d14

Young, A. (2021, February 1). *Reprogramming your subconscious mind: A step-by-step guide*. Rainmakers. https://gorainmakers.com/2021/02/01/reprogramming-your-subconscious-mind-a-step-by-step-guide/

Zapata, K. (2020, December 22). *Exactly how to manifest anything you want or desire*. Oprah Daily. https://www.oprahdaily.com/life/a30244004/how-to-manifest-anything/

Made in the USA
Coppell, TX
26 March 2023